P9-DML-995

Riga
LATVIA

LITHUANIA

SOVIET UNION

POLAND

Warsaw

AUSCHWITZ-BIRKENAU

CZECHOSLOVAKIA

Vienna

HUNGARY

Budapest

RUMANIA

YUGOSLAVIA

Belgrade

Other places

Basel

In 1933, Alice Frank-Stern, Anne's grandmother, moved to Basel from Frankfurt am Main. After the war, Anne's father also went to live there.

Osnabrück

The Van Pels family, who went into hiding in the Secret Annexe with the Frank family, originally came from Osnabrück. They fled to Amsterdam in 1937.

The countries on this map have the 1939 borders. After the Second World War the borders of some of the countries were changed.

Anne Frank

Anne Frank

Anne Frank House

Ruud van der Rol
Rian Verhoeven

Authors
Ruud van der Rol
Rian Verhoeven

Photographic research
Yt Stoker

Design
Erik Uitenbogaard (B&U)

Photography
Allard Bovenberg
Kees Rutten
Maarten van de Velde

Maps and drawings of the Secret Annexe
Gerard de Groot

Translation
Tony Langham
Plym Peters

Production
Anneke Boekhoudt
Nico de Bruijn
Jan Buning

Lithography
B&R Lithografen, Utrecht

With thanks to:
David Barnouw, *Netherlands State Institute for War Documentation*
Karen Beijer
Janrense Boonstra
Anki Duin
Miep Gies
Yoeri de Graaf
Sonja Lukkenaer
Inge Luttikhuizen
Trudie van Nimwegen
Karen Peters
Marie-José Rijnders
Wouter van der Sluis
Juliëtte Smink
Dineke Stam
Tim Steinweg
Anna Westra
Hans Westra

With special thanks to
Joke Kniesmeyer.
Her expertise and her great dedication were invaluable in the creation of this book.

Published by:
LRV-info, Kampen, the Netherlands

© Anne Frank Stichting
   Amsterdam, 1992, 5th print
All rights reserved. No part of this publication may be reproduced, stored into a computer information file or published in any form or by any means, either electronic, photocopying, recording or otherwise without the prior written permission of the publishers and the Anne Frank Stichting. Insofar as making copies from this publication is permitted on the basis of article 16B of Copyright Act 1912j°, the Decree of 10 June 1974, Stb. 351, as amended by the Decree of 23 August 1985, Stb. 471, and article 17 of the Copyright Act of 1912, the reimbursement legally required for this must be paid to the Stichting Reprorecht (Postbox 882, 1180 AW Amstelveen, the Netherlands). For the reproduction of part(s) of this publication in anthologies, readers and other compilations (article 16 of the Copyright Act 1912), please contact the publisher and the Anne Frank Stichting.

ISBN 90 384 0497 2
NUGI 213

Table of contents

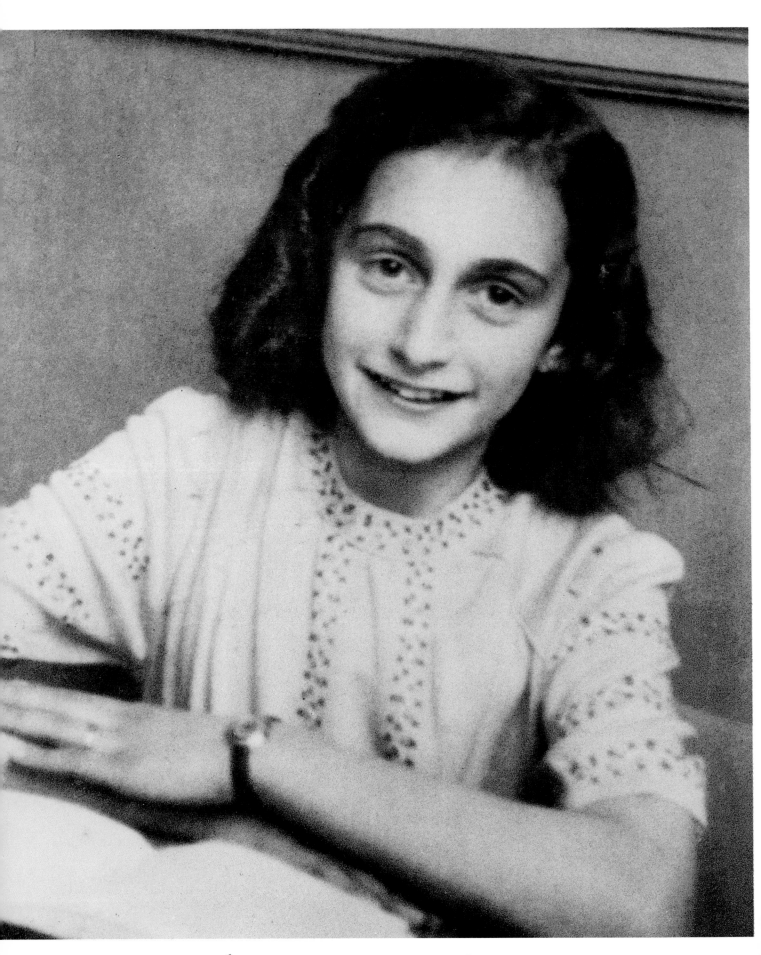

The best birthday present

Anne Frank woke early at six 'o clock in the morning on Friday 12 June. This was quite understandable, because it was her birthday. She was thirteen years old. She could hardly wait to get up.

Anne lived with her father and mother, and sister Margot, who was three years older than her, in a newly built area of Amsterdam.

It was 1942, and it was wartime. The Netherlands had been occupied by the Germans for two years. The Frank family was Jewish. The Germans discriminated against the Jews and persecuted them. It was becoming increasingly difficult for Jews to lead ordinary lives, but Anne was not thinking about that on her birthday.

At seven o' clock she went to her parents' bedroom. Then the whole family gathered together in the living-room to unwrap the presents.

That day, Anne was given a lot of presents: books, a jig-saw puzzle, a brooch, sweets, and many other things. Her parents gave her a diary that morning. The diary had a hard cover with a red and white check pattern. Anne was delighted with it. It was her best present. She had never had a diary before. Anne had many friends, both boys and girls, but with them she talked only about everyday things. Anne decided that she would pretend her diary was her very best friend, a friend she could trust with everything. She called her: 'Kitty'. On the first page of her diary, Anne wrote:

Ik zal hoop ik aan jou alles kunnen toevertrouwen, zoals ik het nog aan niemand gekund heb, en ik hoop dat je een grote steun voor me zult zijn.
Anne Frank. 12 Juni 1942.

I hope I shall be able to confide in you completely, as I have never been able to do in anyone before, and I hope that you will be a great support and comfort to me. (12 June 1942).

On the inside of the cover she stuck a photograph of herself, and wrote next to it: *Gorgeous photo, isn't it!!!*

Anne started writing in her diary two days later, on Sunday 14 June. Of course, she had no idea that soon afterwards her life was to change completely. For more than two years Anne wrote in her diary about all the things that happened to her.

On that day, she had no idea either that later, millions of people throughout the world would read her diary.

From Frankfurt to Amsterdam

Anne Frank was born in the German city of Frankfurt am Main on 12 June 1929. Her father, Otto Frank, took this photograph the next day. Anne's mother was called Edith Frank-Holländer.
Otto Frank was a keen photographer. He took many photographs, especially of his children, and started a photograph album for Anne.

The members of the family soon came to visit and admire the new baby. Of course, Anne's grandmother also came. Otto Frank took a photograph of her, together with her two grandchildren. Anne had an older sister, Margot. Margot was born on 16 February 1926. In this photograph she was three years old.

The Frank family lived on the Marbachweg 307. It was the middle of summer. Just after Anne came home from the hospital, a group photograph was taken on the balcony. Anne can be seen on the lap of Mrs. Dassing, the maternity nurse who came to help when she was born. Mrs. Frank is standing behind her. To the left is Kathi, the Frank family's housekeeper, with Margot. There are also three little girls, neighbours who came to see Anne, on the photograph.

When Anne was born, her parents had been married for four years. They were married on 12 May 1925 in the synagogue* in Aachen. Otto was 36 years old and Edith was 25. The newly wed couple went on their honeymoon to Italy. They stayed in several places, including San Remo on the Mediterranean coast.

Otto's mother was Alice Frank-Stern. His father had died in 1909, when Otto was only 20 years old. Otto Frank was born and grew up in Frankfurt am Main. His family had lived in Frankfurt am Main for generations.
Edith Holländer was born in Aachen, very near the Dutch border. For over two years Otto and Edith lived in Otto's mother's house. But in the autumn of 1927 they moved to the house on the Marbachweg.

Otto, Edith and Margot lived on the first two floors in the right half of this house on the Marbachweg 307. They moved because they wanted a house with a garden. Margot was eighteen months old at the time.

9

The Frank family were liberal Jews*. This means that they observed the traditions of the Jewish religion, though they were not strict believers. The Frank family was German, spoke German and read books in German. Reading and studying were very important to Otto Frank, not only for himself, but also for his daughters. This photograph shows Margot in front of his bookcase in 1929.

There were many children living in the neighbourhood. Almost every afternoon children came to play with Margot in the garden. This photograph shows Margot on the far left. Anne later wrote the date above it in her photograph album: *July 1929*. At the time she was still in her cradle.

As soon as Anne was walking, she played with the other children. Just over a year later, in September 1930, Anne can also be seen in a photograph. Here she is shown third from the left, wearing a hat. Margot is seated, third from the right.
The children in the neighbourhood did not all have the same background. Some were Catholic, others Protestant or Jewish. Obviously they were curious about each other's festivals. Margot was invited to the communion celebration* of one of her girlfriends, and when the Frank family celebrated Chanukka*, the neighbours' children were sometimes invited to join in.

There was a sandpit in the garden where Anne liked to play a lot. She had to stay in the garden, but Margot was allowed out of the gate to play with her friends in the street. (1931)

Papa with his sprogs were the words that Anne wrote later in her photograph album (1930). Anne and Margot were crazy about their father. They had their own pet name for Otto Frank: Anne, Margot and Edith usually called him 'Pim'. Later Anne often called her father by this name in her diary.

Before going to bed at night, Otto often told Anne and Margot stories which he made up himself. These were usually about the two Paulas, two girls who were both called Paula: the good Paula, who obeyed her parents, and the naughty Paula, who got up to all sorts of mischief.

At the end of March 1931, the Frank family went to live in the Ganghoferstrasse 24. This was even better and more healthy for the children. There were lovely paths to take walks in the neighbourhood of the house. There were also hills where they could go tobogganing in winter. Anne and Margot continued to see their former neighbours, but also soon made new friends.

In the summer of 1932, Margot (centre) was six years old. Anne (right) was just three.

11

Three days later, 13 March 1933. There had been elections in Frankfurt for the municipal council. The Nazis*, followers of Hitler, had won many votes. They celebrated the victory in front of the town hall, not far from the Hauptwache. They raised their arms in the Hitler salute, screaming: 'Heil Hitler! Heil Hitler! Down with the Jews!'

The Nazis swarmed into the town hall and raised a red flag with a black swastika* on the facade. The mayor was forced to resign and one of the Nazis took his place. The police did not do anything.

These things were happening in many towns in Germany.

It was 10 March 1933. The worst of the winter cold had passed. Anne and Margot are seen wearing knee-length stockings, though they still have on their thick winter coats. The Frank family are on their way into town to go shopping. Otto Frank took this photograph on the Hauptwache, a famous square in the centre of Frankfurt am Main.

That winter there had been many changes for the Frank family, and for all other Jews in Germany. Six weeks earlier, in January, Adolf Hitler had come into power. Otto and Edith were very worried, but they did not show it to the children.

MRZ. 10 1933

The Tietz department store was very close to the Hauptwache. There was a photograph booth there. This photograph shows Anne, Margot and their mother together. Apart from giving the date, it also shows how much they weighed together: almost 110 kilos. It is one of the last photographs taken of the Frank family in Frankfurt am Main.

12

Adolf Hitler gains power

Things were very bad in Germany in 1929, the year in which Anne Frank was born. There was a great deal of poverty and unemployment. Most Germans were very dissatisfied. The German National Socialist Labour Party, the NSDAP*, attracted increasing numbers of followers. The leader of this party was called Adolf Hitler and his followers were called Nazis.

Hitler said that the Germans were really a sort of super race. He thought that true Germans were the best, strongest and most intelligent people in the whole world. That is why Hitler thought the German people had the right to conquer and enslave other nations. He promised the German people a beautiful future.

On the night of 9-10 November 1938, Nazis throughout Germany destroyed synagogues and Jewish shops. They set fire to many buildings and smashed windows. That night is known as the 'Kristallnacht'*. In the days that followed, about 30,000 Jewish men and boys were rounded up and taken to concentration camps*.

Adolf Hitler, the Nazi leader, making a speech.

Why was it that there was so much poverty and unemployment in Germany? According to Hitler, it was the fault of the Jews. He maintained that Jews were dangerous. He screamed that all Jews were bad, mean and dishonest. By saying this he was confirming a feeling of anti-semitism*, another word for the hatred of Jews.

Hitler did not invent anti-semitism. It existed long before Hitler came into power and it still exists today, in our own time, in Germany, Great Britain and other countries.

Many Germans rather liked the idea that they were better than all the other people. And it was quite convenient to blame the Jews for all the problems.

So many people voted for Hitler that the NSDAP became the largest party. In 1933, Hitler became the leader of the government. The real aim of the Nazis became clear. They destroyed democracy and banned all parties except the NSDAP. Anyone who dared to oppose them was beaten up or thrown into prison. The prisons were soon full and concentration camps* were established. Many Germans kept quiet because they were afraid. But most Germans admired Hitler. They were prepared to blindly believe what Hitler said and simply do what he wanted them to.

Hitler tried to inflame hatred of the Jews. He did this in all sorts of ways: on the radio, in the newspapers, in films, etc. Life became increasingly difficult for Jews. Men and women lost their jobs, and at school Jewish children had to sit separately. And this was only the beginning.

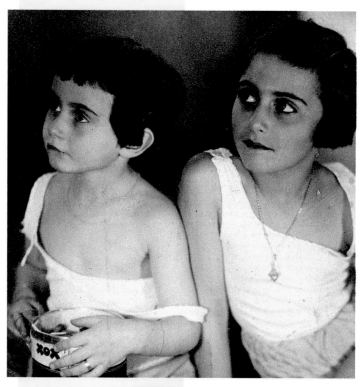

1933: Anne and Margot stayed with their grandmother in Aachen, together with Edith Frank. They no longer lived in Frankfurt am Main. The Frank family had decided to leave Germany because Hitler was taking more and more measures against the Jews. Jews in Germany were afraid of the future.

The Frank family decided to move to the Netherlands. Otto Frank received an offer to start a new company in Amsterdam. These photographs were taken by a photographer in Aachen. They were probably sent to Otto Frank, who had already been in Amsterdam for a few months to start the business and look for a new house.

Anne's other grandmother, Otto Frank's mother, also left Germany in 1933. She went to Switzerland, where some of her family lived already.

This photo dates from 1936. It shows some of the family on the station in Basel (Switzerland). Alice Frank-Stern, Anne's grandmother, is standing on the far left. Erich Elias, an uncle, is standing on the right, and next to him, Leni Elias-Frank, an aunt. Between them are two of Anne's cousins, Bernd and Stephan.

Fleeing to another country

The Frank family left Germany when Hitler came into power. Otto Frank was not the only one who was worried about the events in his country. Thousands of other people tried to escape from Germany once the Nazis had taken power. They suspected that for them life would become even more intolerable. There were also people who thought that everything would be allright in the end, and wanted to wait and see what happened. But the Nazis went on introducing measures. Opponents were put in prison. More and more laws were passed making life impossible for Jews: step by step they were deprived of their work, their money and their freedom.

In the next few years, thousands of Jews tried to escape abroad. But this became more difficult every day. They needed money for the journey. The country where they were going usually demanded that Jews who wanted to go there either had work there already or otherwise had a lot of money. Many people were unable to meet these conditions.

Other countries were increasingly reluctant to accept refugees from Germany. Furthermore, they thought that the stories about persecution and the concentration camps were

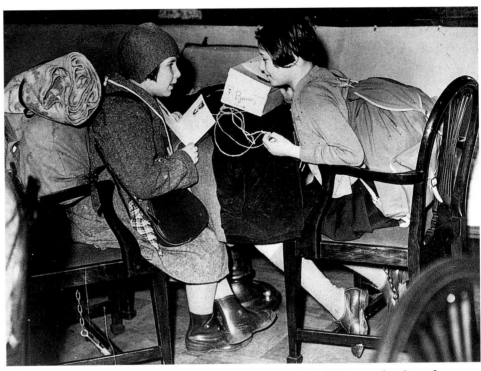

Jewish children on their way to England. Many parents sent their children on ahead to safer countries. The parents themselves were often not admitted and had to stay in Germany.

exaggerated. Their governments issued all sorts of regulations to stop the refugees at the borders. Some countries even stopped admitting refugees altogether.

Nevertheless, there were many Jews who managed to flee the country. In 1933, there were about 600,000 Jews living in Germany. Between 1933 and 1939, about half of them managed to leave.

The rest remained in Germany. These were people who had no money, were too old and weak to travel, or were not admitted to any other country. Their lives were made increasingly difficult. The Nazis humiliated them on the streets and at school, and removed their rights one by one, until they finally had no rights at all.

The station in Naarden. These Jewish refugees have just arrived in the Netherlands.

1929 - 1942

In the autumn of 1933, Otto Frank found a suitable home in Amsterdam: the second floor of a house on the Merwedeplein. It was a recently built area and the house of the Frank family was new. The trees and shrubs in the square were still small.

Edith and Margot went to Amsterdam in December, but Anne stayed with her grandmother for a while until the house was completely furnished. Nine years later, Anne wrote about this in her diary. ... *I went to the Netherlands in February, where I was put on the table for Margot as a birthday present.*

They lived in this house until they had to go into hiding. The house of the Frank family is coloured in red.

In 1934, many new houses were being built in the area. This was fun for the children, as there was a great deal of sand to play in. Anne was now five years old. The Frank family liked living in Amsterdam. There were several other Jews who had fled from Germany living in their area.

1934: One of the advantages of Amsterdam is that it was not far from the beach. The Frank family regularly went to Zandvoort aan Zee on their days off and during the holidays.

This photograph shows Anne, Margot and their mother Edith on the beach in the summer of 1934. Mrs. Schneider is sitting in the beach chair. She was Otto Frank's secretary in Frankfurt.

16

Anne played a lot with her friends out in the street. There were still very few cars about, so it was not dangerous. In this photograph, Anne (right) and her friends are standing on the pavement of the square. It was 1936, and Anne was seven years old. The two friends were called Eva Goldberg (left) and Sanne Ledermann (centre).

Anne went to school from 1934. First she went to the infant class of the Montessori school for two years. This school was very near the Merwedeplein. Margot also went to this school. This photograph shows Anne in the class of Mr. Van Gelder. She was seven years old and was reading and writing quite well.

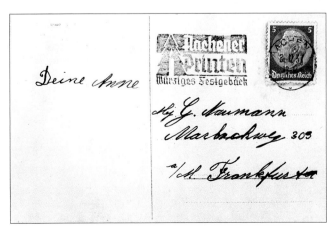

As soon as Anne and Margot could write, they sent letters abroad. They would send a card or a letter to their family for birthdays or other events, and they also wrote to their former neighbour in Frankfurt am Main, and to Kathi, who had been their housekeeper. This is a card sent by Anne to her former neighbour Gertrud in 1937. Anne was visiting her grandmother in Aachen at the time. She remembered that Gertrud did not know any Dutch, and wrote 'Deine Anne' ('Your Anne').

In 1933, Otto Frank started his new business. His company was called Opekta Werke, and it sold pectin. Pectin is a fruit powder which you need to make jam. Many people made their own jam because it was much cheaper and nicer than shop-bought jam. Pectin is sold in bottles, boxes and paper bags.

This is the label of a bottle. House-wives who had questions about making jam could telephone the Opekta information service. They would talk to Miep Santrouschitz. Miep worked at Otto's office. After the summer of 1937 she was assisted by Bep Voskuijl.

Miep Santrouschitz and Otto Frank. A friendship soon grew up between Miep and the Frank family. Miep and her fiancé, Jan Gies, regularly visited them. Miep and Otto talked a great deal about everything that was happening in Germany. Miep was also fiercely against Hitler and the Nazis.

Anne sometimes visited her father's office. This photograph shows her on the pavement in front of the office. She often talked to Miep about films, because Anne was very keen on films and filmstars.

1936: Otto Frank's business was advertised. This car drove through the streets so that everyone could see what Opekta was.

In 1938, a second company was established: Pectacon B.V. This company sold herbs for flavouring meat. Hermann van Pels was Otto's partner. The Van Pels family had fled from the German city of Osnabrück to the Netherlands a year earlier. They had one son, Peter. This photograph shows Peter (centre) in Osnabrück in 1935 or 1936 when he was eight or nine years old.

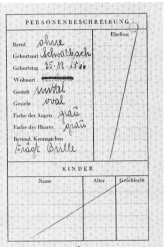

The Frank family went to the photographer nearly every year to have a sheet of photographs taken with a lot of different passport photographs. There are dozens of photographs on every sheet. These are Margot's in 1939.

Margot was quieter than Anne and listened to her parents more attentively. She also looked after her clothes better, unlike Anne. For this reason Margot was often held up as an example to Anne. Sometimes Anne was jealous of Margot because she was so good at school, but also because some people said that Margot was the more beautiful and the more intelligent of the two girls.

Grandmother Holländer's passport. Grandmother Holländer came from Aachen to live with the Frank family in March 1939. In Germany the situation had become almost intolerable for the Jews. There was enormous hatred and violence against them. It was a miracle that Grandmother Holländer was allowed to enter the Netherlands. Many Jewish refugees were sent back at the border. Granny was ill and weak, and spent a great deal of time in bed.

There are also sheets of photographs of Anne. These are a number of individual photographs (from left to right:

May 1935, December 1935, 1939, 1940). Later she used these photographs to decorate her diary.

This photograph of Anne was taken somewhere in the street in 1939. Anne liked laughing, history, filmstars, Greek mythology, writing, cats, dogs, and boys. She had a large circle of boyfriends and girlfriends. She liked going to parties and to the ice-cream parlour 'Oase' in the quarter where she lived. Every day she cycled to school, where she talked a great deal. She was regularly given extra work as a punishment for talking.

The Frank family still often went to the beach. Anne later stuck this photograph in her diary and wrote underneath: *This is June 1939. (...) Margot and I were just coming out of the water and I remember that I was really cold. That is why I put on my towelling robe. Granny is sitting in the background, so dear and quiet, as she used to sit so often (...)*
This was one of the last times that Margot and Anne went to the beach. On 10 May 1940, the German army unexpectedly entered the Netherlands. The Frank family had hoped to be safe there, but the German army had caught up with them. It was not possible to flee any further.

19

The Netherlands are occupied, the persecution begins

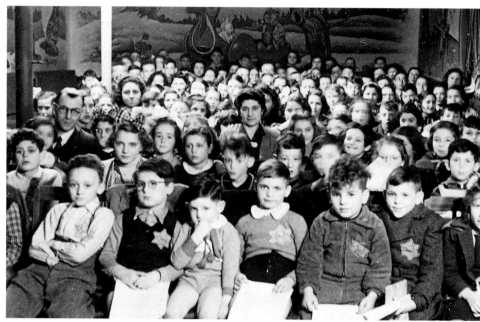

While the Frank family lived a fairly trouble-free life in the Netherlands, Hitler and his supporters went ahead with their plans in Germany. From 1933, Hitler was getting ready for war. In 1938, the Nazis occupied Austria and parts of Czechoslovakia. When the Germans invaded Poland in September 1939, England and France declared war on Germany.

The German army went on. On 10 May 1940, they invaded the Netherlands. The Royal Family and the Dutch Government fled to England. Four days later, on 14 May, the Germans bombed Rotterdam. Many people were killed. When the Nazis threatened to bomb other cities as well, the Netherlands surrendered.

After the first few weeks of shock and panic, daily life for most people was fairly nor-

From May 1942, all Jews aged six and above had to wear a yellow Star of David* on their clothes. In this way everyone could see who was Jewish.

Germany in 1942

German allies

German occupied territories

Other countries in Europe were also occupied. The Germans did not succeed in conquering England. Hitler also invaded countries in North Africa and the Soviet Union. Nazi Germany was supported by Italy and Japan. Germany's enemies joined together. They were known as the Allies*: the United States, England, France and the Soviet Union.

Throughout the Netherlands there were signs saying 'Forbidden for Jews'.

mal. They went to work and went to school as usual. In the first year of the war, the occupation did not yet have much effect.

The Germans wanted to know who was Jewish, and for this purpose every Dutch person had to be registered at the end of 1940, indicating whether they were Jewish or not. Anyone who failed to do so risked severe punishment. In November 1940, all Jewish civil servants were dismissed. The following year all Dutchmen were given identity cards.

This was a sort of passport. The cards of Jews were stamped with a 'J'. This was soon followed by all sorts of laws prohibiting many things for the Jews, step by step, one measure after another, just like in Germany.

How did the non-Jewish population in the Netherlands react? Most people did not interfere at all. Some were afraid. Others did not think that these measures were serious enough to oppose. They hoped that the war would soon be over.

Many non-Jewish Dutch people no longer associated with Jews. They thought it was too dangerous. That was exactly what the Germans wanted. They wished to separate the Jews from the rest of the population so that the Jews would be more and more isolated. More and more measures were passed against them. In the end, Jews were no longer allowed to do anything.

But why were the Germans doing all these things? What was their plan? This was a carefully kept secret.

To Anne and Margot and all the other Jews in the Netherlands, the German occupation did not seem too bad. In 1940, they went to school as usual and had fun with their friends. The newspapers were full of articles insulting and taunting Jews, but Otto and Edith tried to keep this from their daughters as much as possible.

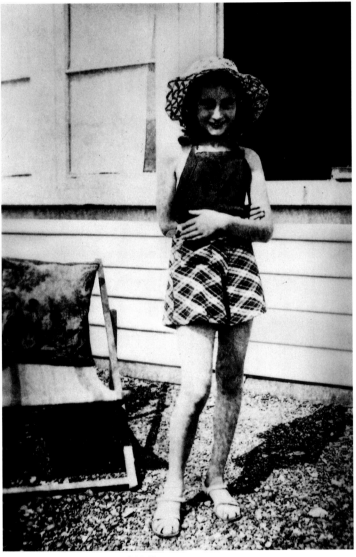

One year later, the summer of 1940. Anne is on the flat roof at the back of their house. She often sat there to read when it was good weather. Holland was occupied. You didn't really notice much, except that foreign soldiers walked through the streets. Usually they behaved impeccably. All sorts of measures were being prepared against the Jews in secret, but no one knew anything about these yet.

On 1 December 1940, Otto Frank's business moved to new premises: Prinsengracht 263. This photograph taken in 1941 shows the office staff. Front left is Victor Kugler, with Bep Voskuijl next to him and Miep Santrouschitz on the right. In the background, Esther is standing and Pine is seated. They only worked in the office for a short while.

By now, the Netherlands had been occupied by the Germans for almost six months. Otto knew what had happened in Germany. Jews had soon been stopped from owning a business there. He expected this to happen in the Netherlands too. For this reason he transferred his business to Victor Kugler and Johannes Kleiman. The business was also renamed in 1941: Handelsvereniging Gies & Co.

21

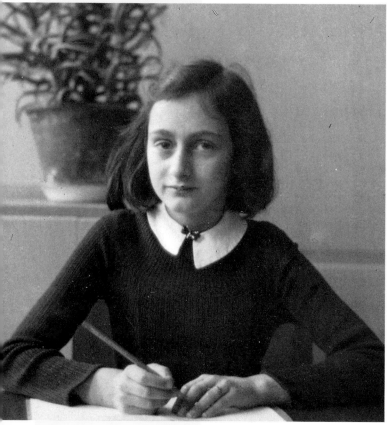

Anne on the balcony of their house on the Merwedeplein in May 1941. Anne later wrote under this photograph in her album: *Granny was supposed to be on the photograph. Margot pressed down the shutter and when it was developed we saw that Granny had disappeared.*

Anne at the Montessori school, in 1941. This was her last year at primary school. After the summer holidays in 1941, Jewish children heard that they would no longer be allowed to go to the school of their choice. In future, Jews had to go to a Jewish school with only Jewish teachers, separately from their non-Jewish peers. Anne and Margot then went to the 'Jewish High School'.

But this was not all. Anne later wrote in her diary: *Anti-Jewish decrees followed each other in quick succession and our freedom was strictly limited. Jews must wear a yellow star: Jews must hand in their bicycles. Jews are banned from trams and are forbidden to use any car, even a private one; Jews are only allowed to do their shopping between three and five o' clock; Jews may only use Jewish barbers; Jews must be indoors from eight o' clock in the evening until six o' clock in the morning; (...). But life went on in spite of it all, so we could not do this and we were forbidden to do that. Jacque used to say to me: 'You're scared to do anything, because it may be forbidden'.*

On 16 July 1941, Miep married Jan Gies. The Frank family was also invited to the wedding. This photograph shows Otto and Anne walking amongst the other wedding guests. Edith Frank had stayed at home because Granny Holländer was very ill. Granny did not live long. Anne wrote: *In the summer of 1941 Granny Holländer fell very ill. (...) she had to have an operation, and my birthday didn't mean much. (...) Granny died in January 1942; no one will ever know how much she is present in my thoughts and how much I love her still.*

It was June 1942.
It is boiling hot, we are all positively melting, and in this heat I have to walk everywhere. Now I can fully appreciate how nice a tram is; but that is a forbidden luxury for Jews - shank's mare is good enough for us. (...) We are allowed on the ferry and that is about all. There is a little boat from the Jozef Israëlskade, the man there took us at once when we asked him.

Anne and Margot often played ping-pong with their friends. Usually they went to have an ice-cream afterwards in one of the ice-cream parlours where Jews were still allowed.

VAKKEN	STAND VAN KENNIS				OPMERKINGEN omtrent vorderingen, vlijt en gedrag. (Deze kolommen worden slechts ingevuld als daartoe bepaalde aanleiding bestaat).			
	1	2	3	4	Eerste rapport	Tweede rapport	Derde rapport	Jaarrapport
Stelkunde	9	8	8	9				
Gonio- en Trigonometrie								
Meetkunde	8	8	9	8				
Beschrijvende Meetkunde								
Mechanica								
Natuurkunde	8	9	8	9				
Scheikunde								
Plant- en Dierkunde	9	9	9	9				
Cosmographie								
Geschiedenis	8	7	8	8				
Staatsinrichting								
Staathuishoudkunde								
Aardrijkskunde	8	7	9	8				
Nederlands	5	7	8	7				
Frans								
Hoogduits	9	8	9	8				
Engels								
Handelswetenschappen	96	96	96	96				
Handtekenen								
Rechtlijnig tekenen								
Lichamelijke oefening	8	8	7	7				
Handwerken	9	8	7	8				

Z.O.Z.

Gezien: *Otto Frank*   Gezien: *Otto Frank*   Gezien: *Otto Frank*   ~~Gezien:~~

The 1941-1942 school year had come to an end. As usual, Margot had a glowing report. This is a photograph of Margot's report of the previous year. Anne's report was also excellent. She had one poor mark for algebra. Anne wrote about this: *My parents are quite different from most, they don't care a bit whether my reports are good or bad, as long as I am well and happy, and not too cheeky, then the rest will come by itself.*
But in reality Anne and Margot's parents were extremely worried about what was going to happen to them and other Jews in the Netherlands in the future.

'Dear Kitty'

This is possibly the last photograph taken of Anne Frank. In 1942, Jews were not allowed to take photographs, but it was not forbidden for them to be photographed. No photographs were taken in the years they spent in hiding. During that period everyone had other things on their minds. Thus the photographs in this chapter were taken either before that period or after the war.

Anne was given her diary on her 13th birthday, on 12 June 1942. She started writing in it two days later.

She wrote about her family, her friends and her school. That month she made a new friend: Hello Silberberg. He was sixteen and Anne thought he was very good-looking. Anne was enjoying life and preferred not to think about the war. But it was dangerous for Jews to be thoughtless. This was made clear, for example, on Monday 29 June. Hello came to visit Anne at home at the end of the afternoon to meet her parents.

Dear Kitty,

I had bought a cream cake, sweets, tea, and fancy biscuits, quite a spread, but neither Hello nor I felt like sitting stiffly side by side indefinitely, so we went for a walk, and it was already ten past eight when he brought me home. Daddy was very cross, and thought it was very wrong of me because it is dangerous for Jews to be out after eight o' clock, and I had to promise to be in by ten to eight in future. (1 July 1942)

Her father was often at home during the day. Anne thought it must be very difficult for him to feel so superfluous. In the same week, at the beginning of July, her father had a serious talk with her.

When we walked across our little square together a few days ago, Daddy began to talk of us going into hiding, he is very worried that it will be very difficult for us to live completely cut off from the world. I asked him why on earth he was beginning to talk of that already. 'Yes Anne', he said, 'you know that we have been taking food, clothes, furniture to other people for more than a year now.' (5 July 1942)

It's an odd idea for someone like me to keep a diary; not only because I have never done so before, but because it seems to me that neither I - nor for that matter, anyone else - will be interested in the unbosomings of a thirteen-year-old schoolgirl.
(20 June 1942)

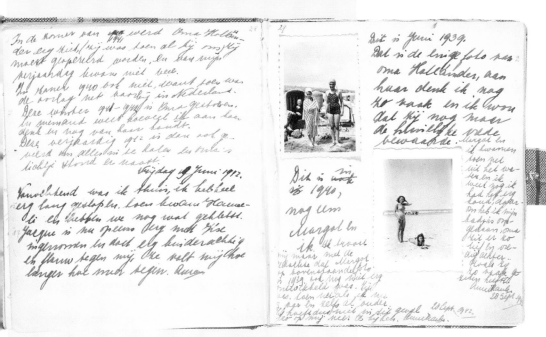

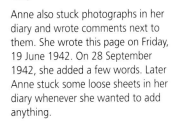

Anne also stuck photographs in her diary and wrote comments next to them. She wrote this page on Friday, 19 June 1942. On 28 September 1942, she added a few words. Later Anne stuck some loose sheets in her diary whenever she wanted to add anything.

Anne on the flat roof of their house on the Merwedeplein in 1940.

'We don't want our belongings to be seized by the Germans, but we certainly don't want to fall into their clutches ourselves. So we shall disappear of our own accord, and not wait until they come and fetch us.'

'But, Daddy, when will it be?' He spoke so seriously that I grew very anxious. 'Don't you worry about it, we shall arrange everything. Make the most of your carefree young life while you can.' (5 July 1942).

That is all Otto Frank said. Anne just hoped it would never happen!

Anne wrote those words in her diary on Sunday morning, 5 July. But things went wrong that very day.

It was a swelteringly hot summer's day. The bell rang at three o' clock in the afternoon. Anne did not hear it because she was being lazy, lying in a chair on the verandah, reading. A little later, Margot came to Anne excitedly.

'The SS* have sent a call-up notice for Daddy', she whispered. (...) It was a great shock to me, a call-up; everyone knows what that means. I picture concentration camps and lonely cells -should we let him be doomed to this? 'Of course he won't go', declared Margot, while we waited together. 'Mummy has gone to the Van Daans[1] to discuss whether we should move into our hiding place tomorrow. The Van Daans are going with us, so we shall be seven in all.' (8 July 1942)

[1] Anne gave a couple of people false names. More information on p. 63.

The evening before going into hiding, Otto wrote a postcard to his sister Leni Elias-Frank in Switzerland. Otto hinted that the family was going into hiding. He wrote: 'It is a pity that we can no longer correspond with you, but that is how it is. You must understand.' Edith, Margot and Anne also sent their regards. Anne wrote: 'I cannot write a letter about the holidays now. Regards and kisses from Anne.'

A little later Anne and Margot were still in their bedroom, frightened and shocked. Then suddenly Margot told Anne that the summons was not for their father but for herself !

I was more frightened than ever and began to cry. Margot is 16, would they really take girls of that age away alone? (8 July 1942).

But fortunately she did not go, because the Frank family went into hiding*. Into hiding .... but when, how and where? These were the questions which Anne asked herself over and over again.

Anne took her satchel and started to pack it. First her diary, then her curlers, handkerchiefs, school books, comb and a few letters. *(....) I put in the craziest things with the idea that we were going into hiding, but I am not sorry, memories mean more to me than dresses.* (8 July 1942).

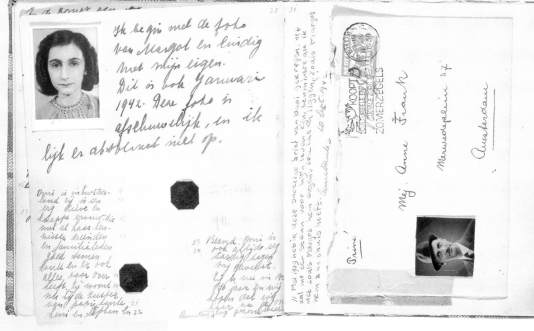

Anne used two sorts of writing in her diary. Sometimes she wrote in block letters, but she also often used joined together, cursive writing. In cursive writing, Anne wrote next to her photograph: *I started with Margot's photograph and finished with my own. This is January 1942. This photograph is horrible and I look absolutely nothing like it.*

Otto Frank had informed Miep Gies several weeks before about the plans to go into hiding. Otto knew he could trust her. He thought very carefully about asking Miep whether she would help the Frank family to go into hiding. She said that of course she would, although she knew that it would be very dangerous.

Miep Gies was fetched at the end of the afternoon. Miep came and took some shoes, dresses, coats, underclothes and stockings. She came again at eleven o' clock in the evening with her husband Jan. Again she took a lot of things.

Anne wrote: *I was dog-tired and although I knew it would be my last night in my own bed, I fell asleep immediately (....).* (8 July 1942).

Anne was awakened by her mother on Monday morning, 6 July at half past five.

Deportation of the Jews from the Netherlands

On Monday, 29 June 1942, all the Dutch newspapers announced that the German occupiers had decided to deport the Jews to labour camps in Germany. The Jews in the Netherlands panicked: what would happen to them? What could they do? After all, the German occupiers had recorded all the names and addresses of the Jews. Many Jews thought about going into hiding, but this was very difficult.

On Sunday, 5 July, the first thousand Jews in the Netherlands received a card. Margot Frank belonged to this first group. The card stated that they were to report to a particular address. There they were given a form stating when their train was leaving and what they had to take with them. The Jews knew only that they were first being sent to the camp at Westerbork by train. No one knew what would happen to them after that.

In 1942 and 1943, the Germans called up all the Jews in the Netherlands for deportation*, but many of them did not turn up. Then the German police adopted a tougher approach. They often turned up at the door unannounced, and took people with them. They also carried out raids*: they would seal off a whole area, and round up all the Jews. People were dragged from their homes, loaded onto lorries, and taken to Westerbork by train.

The Germans were helped to a large extent by the Dutch police. There were also Dutch Nazis who helped the Germans. When they entered Jewish homes they often first stole everything of value: money, jewellery and food. By the end of September 1943, nearly all the Jews in the Netherlands had been rounded up. Then the Germans made greater efforts to trace the Jews who had gone into hiding. Even more were discovered and taken away.

Jews waiting for transport.

There were groups of 'Jew hunters'. These people were rewarded for every Jew - man, woman or child. This is a receipt. Someone has betrayed five Jews and receives Fl. 37.50 from the German police. This sum was equal to the average weekly salary.

1942 - 1944

Amsterdam

One of the last photographs of Margot. As she was a few years older than Anne, her parents told her about the plans for going into hiding before they told Anne. Unlike Anne, Margot was usually rather quiet and reserved. She also kept a diary when they were in hiding, but it was lost.

© 1992 Stedelijk Beheer Amsterdam

The Frank family left the house on the Merwedeplein on 6 July 1942 very early in the morning. They had lived there for eight years. They had to leave most things behind, including the cat, Moortje. Anne wrote: *(...) Nobody knows how much I think about her; whenever I think about her the tears come to my eyes.* (12 July 1942)

The Frank family walked from the Merwedeplein to the Secret Annexe on the Prinsengracht. Jews were not permitted to use the tram, bus or car. Jews were also forbidden bicycles. Thus Margot, who had left earlier with Miep on a bicycle, had already taken a risk. Anne and her parents walked to the Prinsengracht, a distance of about four kilometres. Anne wrote: *We got sympathetic looks from people on their way to work. You could see by their faces how sorry they were they couldn't offer us a lift. The gaudy yellow star spoke for itself.* (9 July 1942)

We put on heaps of clothes as if we were going to the North Pole, the sole reason being to take clothes with us. No Jew in our situation would have dreamed of going out with a suitcase full of clothing. I had on two vests, three pairs of pants, a dress, on top of that a skirt, jacket, summer coat, two pairs of stockings, lace-up shoes, woolly cap, scarf, and still much more; I was nearly stifled before we started, but no one inquired about that. (8 July 1942)

Miep Gies came to fetch Margot. Margot filled her satchel with school books, took her bicycle from the bicycle rack and rode after Miep. Where were they going? Anne still did not know where the mysterious hiding place was.

At half past seven Anne and her parents also closed the door behind them. She only said goodbye to Moortje the cat. The Frank family left a letter to the neighbours asking them to care for the cat. They left the house in total disarray: breakfast things on the table, the beds unmade. Everything gave the impression that they had left in a panic but they did not care. *(....) we only wanted to get away, only escape and arrive safely, nothing else.* (8 July 1942)

Anne described in her diary what happened next. They left their house and walked through the pouring rain, father, mother and Anne each with a school satchel and a shopping bag stuffed full of things, all mixed up. As Jews were not allowed to use public transport, they had to walk.

28

It was only when they were out in the street that her father and mother gradually told her the whole plan of going into hiding. For months they had moved all sorts of things from their home to the underground address. They had already decided to go into hiding on 16 July, but the whole plan had been pushed forward because of the summons for Margot.

Anne's father told her that the hiding place was in his office. Only Victor Kugler, Johannes Kleiman, Miep Gies and Bep Voskuijl knew about their arrival. Bep's father, Mr. Voskuijl, who worked in the store, only heard about it several weeks later.

When they arrived at the Prinsengracht, Miep quickly took the Frank family upstairs into the Secret Annexe. Then Miep shut the door behind them and they were left alone. Margot was already waiting for them.

Anne looked around her. There were boxes everywhere and piles of bedding. It was an indescribable mess. They started work straight away.

The whole day long we unpacked boxes, filled cupboards, hammered and tidied, until we were dead beat. We sank into clean beds that night. (10 July 1942).

On Tuesday morning they continued with the job where they had stopped the previous day. Anne had hardly any time to think about the great changes in her life. It was not until the next day, Wednesday, that she had a chance to write her diary in detail.

Then I had a chance, for the first time since our arrival, to tell you all about it, and at the same time to realize myself what had actually happened to me and what was still going to happen. (10 July 1942).

The facade of Otto Frank's offices, Prinsengracht 263. The warehouse was on the ground floor (1). Bep's father, Mr. Voskuijl, worked there with two other men. The door furthest on the left (2), led to the storage space on the second and third floors. The door next to it (3) led to the office on the first floor.
There is another door at the top of the stairs, with a frosted glass window in it, which has 'Office' written in black letters across it. This is the large main office, very big, very light, and very full. Bep, Miep and Mr. Kleiman work there in the daytime. (9 July 1942)

Behind this, there was a smaller office where Mr. Van Pels (Van Daan) and Victor Kugler used to work. Now only Victor Kugler worked there. The two top floors were used as storage space.
Behind this house there was another house, which could not be seen from the road, the Secret Annexe. This house was connected to the Prinsengracht 263 by a small corridor.

Three men worked in the warehouse on the ground floor. This is where the spices were ground, weighed and packed. Only one of them, Bep's father, knew about the family in hiding.

This photograph was taken just after the war. It shows the Secret Annexe (yellow) and the house at the front (red). On the photograph you can see the small window in the attic through which Anne often looked outside. She could see the Westertoren. Through another attic window at the back she looked out onto a chestnut tree (green), amongst other things. Anne wrote about this chestnut tree in her diary several times.

This is the Secret Annexe photographed from the gardens at the back. On the right you can see the branches of the chestnut tree.

1 Anne's room, which she first shared with Margot and later with Fritz Pfeffer (Albert Dussel).

2 The room of Mr. and Mrs. Frank. Later Margot joined them.

3 The room of Mr. and Mrs. Van Pels (Van Daan). The families also cooked and ate together in this room.

4 The food supplies were stored in the attic. Later it was Anne's favourite place to sit quietly and look out of the window.

5 Otto Frank's private office. It was not part of the hiding place, but belonged to the office on the Prinsengracht 263.

6 The kitchen. The kitchen was not part of the hiding place. It was used by the office staff.

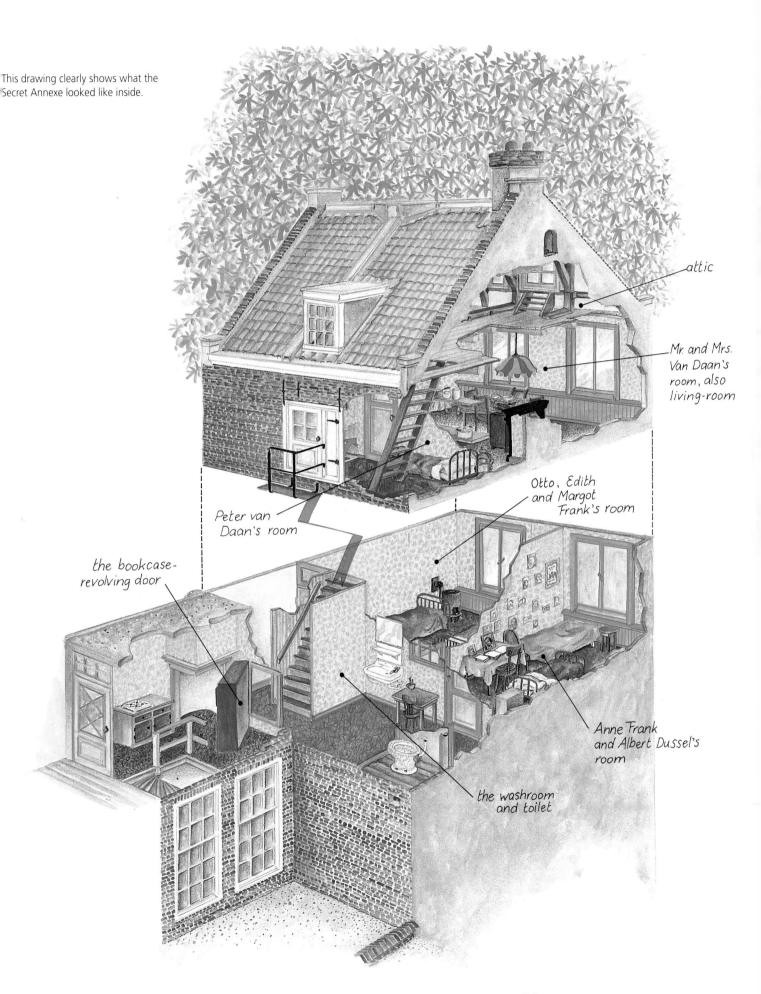

This drawing clearly shows what the Secret Annexe looked like inside.

attic

Mr. and Mrs. Van Daan's room, also living-room

Otto, Edith and Margot Frank's room

Peter van Daan's room

the bookcase-revolving door

Anne Frank and Albert Dussel's room

the washroom and toilet

31

Anne and Margot's room.
Our little room looked very bare at first with nothing on the walls; but thanks to Daddy, who had brought my picture postcards and filmstar collection on beforehand, and with the aid of paste-pot and brush, I have transformed the walls into one gigantic picture. This makes it look much more cheerful (...) (11 July 1942)
Anne wrote most of her diary at the table in her room. This photograph was taken after the war. The room was temporarily furnished in accordance with the instructions of Otto Frank and Miep Gies. Now the room is actually empty. Also see page 58.

The families hiding in the Secret Annexe were completely dependent on their helpers. They all worked in the office and were close colleagues of Otto Frank.
From left to right: Miep Gies, Johannes Kleiman, Otto Frank, Victor Kugler, and Bep Voskuijl.

In the next few days Anne explored every inch of the hiding place.

They were all really scared of being discovered.

During the daytime they walked about quietly and talked softly because the people in the store must not hear them. They also had to take care to make sure that the neighbours could not hear or see them.

We made curtains straightaway on the first day, really one can hardly call them curtains, they are just light, loose strips of material, all different shapes, quality and pattern, which Daddy and I sewed together in a most unprofessional way. These works of art are fixed in position with drawing pins, not to come down again until we emerge from here. (11 July 1942)

The only contact with the outside world took place through Miep Gies, Bep Voskuijl, Victor Kugler and Johannes Kleiman. They bought food, brought books and told them what was happening in Amsterdam. The world had become very small for Anne Frank: a few rooms and an attic window through which she could look at the sky and at the Westertoren. She wrote in her diary: *I can't tell you how oppressive it is never to be able to go outdoors, also I am very afraid that we will be discovered and shot.* (28 September 1942)

Anne was very glad when the Van Pels family joined them on 13 July 1942. In her diary she gave them a different name: the Van Daan family. There were three members of the Van Daan family: Mr. and Mrs. Van Daan and their son Peter, who was fifteen years old. Peter had brought along his cat, Moushi.

The Van Daans arrived on July 13. We thought they were coming on the fourteenth, between the thirteenth and sixteenth of July the Germans called up people right and left which created more and more unrest, so they played for safety, better a day too early than a day too late. (14 August 1942)

Going into hiding

Many Jews tried to escape German deportation by going into hiding. However, it was very difficult to go into hiding. Where could they go? At the start of the war there were not yet any organizations to help people to hide. It was necessary to have non-Jewish friends or acquaintances who were prepared to hide you. But as a result of all the measures introduced by the Germans, most Jews no longer had these friends and acquaintances.

It hardly ever happened that a whole family could hide in one place. In this respect, the Frank family was a great exception. Sometimes parents gave their children to complete strangers, as it was easier to find a place for children to hide than for adults. A child could easily pass for a cousin from the city.

It was difficult enough to find a place to go into hiding, but this was by no means all. Going into hiding cost money. Often people asked the Jews for a lot of money for their keep. Many Jews were poor and could not afford this.

Going into hiding was very dangerous. People who were caught knew that they would be sent to a concentration camp. There were

Several thousand Jewish children were saved. Many found a place to hide with farmers in the countryside. Most of them never saw their parents again.

also many Jews who did not wish to put their non-Jewish helpers in danger, and therefore decided not to go into hiding. The punishment for helping people to go into hiding was very severe. Fortunately, there were still many people who helped the Jews.

These helpers were usually the only contact with the outside world. They provided food, brought newspapers and books, and tried to find a doctor who could be trusted when anyone fell ill. They encouraged and reassured the people in hiding. Helping in this way was a heavy responsibility, full of risks. Many helpers were picked up by the Germans and sent to concentration camps.

It was not until the summer of 1943 that a secret organization was set up to help people in hiding, but by this time the great majority of Jews had been deported.

Of the 140,000 Jews in the Netherlands, about 25,000 eventually went into hiding. Of these, it is estimated that 16,000 survived the war. The other 9,000 were discovered in the end and deported. This was often because they were betrayed.

Many people in hiding did not have such a good hiding place as the Frank family. These people are hiding underneath the floorboards of a house.

1942 - 1944

The room of Mr. and Mrs. Van Pels (Van Daan)
If you go up the next flight of stairs and open the door, you are simply amazed that there could be such a big, light room in such an old house by the canal. There is a stove in this room (...) and a sink. This is now the kitchen (as well as bedroom) for the Van Daan couple, besides being general living room, dining room, and scullery. (9 July 1942)
The families spent a great deal of their time in hiding in this room. The rubbish was burned in the stove. In the summer they did not do this until it was dark, as one of the neighbours might have become suspicious if they had seen smoke coming from the chimney.
This room was also temporarily furnished for the photograph in accordance with directions from Otto Frank and Miep Gies. The room is now empty.

Peter van Pels.
Anne changed his last name in her diary. She described Peter's arrival in the Secret Annexe as follows: *At nine-thirty in the morning (we were still having breakfast) Peter arrived, the Van Daans' son, not sixteen yet, a rather soft, shy, gawky youth; can't expect much from his company.* (14 August 1942)

Anne was glad they were there. It was more fun and a bit less quiet, for the quiet made her rather nervous.

Days passed. Days turned into weeks and months. During the daytime when the staff was working, the families in hiding could only whisper and had to walk around very softly in stockinged feet. No one in the Secret Annexe was allowed to use a tap or toilet between nine o'clock in the morning and seven o'clock in the evening.

We are as quiet as baby mice. Who, three months ago, would have guessed that quicksilver Anne would have to sit still for hours - and what's more, could? (1 October 1942)

What did Anne do during those long hours in the daytime? She studied a lot from the large pile of schoolbooks which had been taken along. Margot and Peter also spent many hours doing schoolwork every day. Mr. Frank helped them and tested them on the lessons. None of the children wanted to fall behind at school. They still hoped that they would be able to go back soon. Anne read many books which Miep brought for her, and she learned shorthand*.

Many Jews in the Netherlands were picked up during these months and taken to the concentration camps. The Frank and Van Daan families escaped this by hiding in the Secret Annexe, but they were on top of each other day and night. They saw and heard everything everyone did. In addition, they were very frightened of being discovered. This is why everyone was always extremely tense. Thus it was no surprise that they regularly argued and quarrelled.

Hermann and Auguste van Pels. Anne gave them false names in her diary: Mr. and Mrs. Van Daan. Mr. Van Pels had been Otto Frank's partner at the Prinsengracht office for several years. Until 1942 the families had little contact. Anne knew the family, but not very well.

34

When the Frank family moved into the Secret Annexe on 6 July 1942, there was no bookcase, just an ordinary door. Anne wrote: *No one would ever guess that there would be so many rooms hidden behind that plain door painted grey. There's a little step in front of the door, and then you are inside.* (9 July 1942)

For safety's sake it was best to hide the entrance to the Secret Annexe. Over a month later, Anne wrote in her diary:

Dear Kitty,
The entrance to our hiding place has now been properly concealed.
Mr. Kugler thought it would be better to put a cupboard in front of our door (...), but of course it had to be a movable cupboard that can open like a door.
Mr. Voskuijl made the whole thing. (We had already let Mr. Voskuijl into the secret and he can't do enough to help.) If we want to go downstairs, we have to first bend down and then jump. The first three days we were all going about with masses of lumps on our foreheads, because we all knocked ourselves against the low doorway. So Peter has made it as soft as possible by nailing a cloth filled with wood wool against the top of the door. Let's see if that helps! (21 August 1942)

Anne wrote: *(...) Why do grownups quarrel so easily, so much, and over the most idiotic things? Up till now I thought that only children squabbled (...).* (28 September 1942)

Anne also found her 'new' life difficult. She had lost everything: her friends, her school, her freedom... Sometimes she was rebellious and sad, and at nights she often cried. During the day she was different; she was lively and boisterous, and usually quite cheerful. She interfered with everything and everyone, and was always ready with an answer. But Mr. and Mrs. Van Daan thought she was an insolent and badly brought up child. She regularly argued with her mother. Margot was often bad tempered with her, and Peter was not much support either.

Margot and Peter aren't a bit what you would call 'young', they are both so staid and quiet. I show up terribly against them, and am always hearing, 'You don't find Margot and Peter doing that - why don't you just once follow your dear sister's example?' I simply loathe it. (5 February 1943)

Anne felt truly alone and misunderstood. Her diary had become a really good friend.

Most of the time life in the Secret Annexe was boring, but there were also moments of great excitement and great fear. One evening the bell suddenly rang loudly at eight o'clock. Everyone was terribly frightened. Was it the German police, the Gestapo*? Was it the end? Everyone held their breath, but there was no more noise.

Three weeks later, they all had another fright.

Miep and Jan Gies celebrated their first wedding anniversary on 16 July 1942, ten days after the Franks went into hiding. On 18 July the family prepared a festive meal in the Secret Annexe with the food that Miep had bought for them herself. That evening Miep and Jan are guests in the Annexe. Anne made the menus with a great sense of humour. Most dishes were formally described in French. Gravy was described as 'sauce de boeuf' and everyone was allowed just a little, because butter was becoming more and more difficult to obtain.

35

On the landing opposite the bookcase, they suddenly heard the sound of hammering. Everyone immediately stopped talking. A quarter of an hour later, someone knocked on the door of the cupboard. Everyone turned pale. Someone was knocking, pulling and pushing at the cupboard.

Just as I thought my last hour was at hand, we heard Mr. Kleiman's voice say: 'Open the door, it's only me.' (20 October 1942)

Then they heard what was the matter. Johannes Kleiman told them there was a carpenter in the house to check the fire extinguishers, and that he had not had time to warn them. The man had gone downstairs again. It was a great relief. Once again, things had turned out alright.

On Tuesday 10 November 1942, Anne heard that an eighth person was coming to hide with them. (...) *We have always thought that there was quite enough room and food for one more. We were only afraid of giving Kugler and Kleiman more trouble. But now that the appalling stories we hear about Jews are getting even worse, Daddy got hold of the two people who had to decide, and they thought it was an excellent plan. It is just as dangerous for seven as for eight, they said, and quite rightly.* (10 November 1942)

They chose someone they knew and who they thought would fit in well: Fritz Pfeffer. In her diary, Anne called him Albert Dussel.

Victor Kugler (right) and Johannes Kleiman (left) helped the families in hiding whenever they could. Like Miep and Bep, they often visited them in the Secret Annexe during the lunch hour when the staff in the warehouse had gone home. They talked about the practical problems of being in hiding, but they also talked about the political situation and the way things were going with the business.

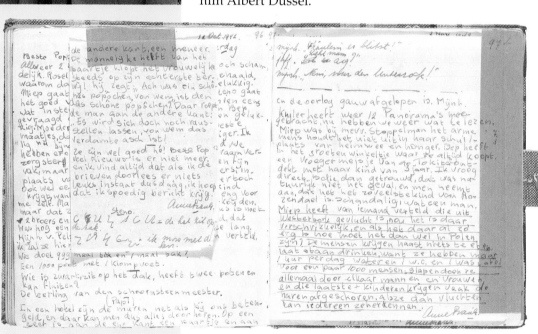

Anne started on a written course of shorthand.
Bep has written to some secretarial school or other and ordered a correspondence course in shorthand for Margot, Peter and me. You wait and see what perfect experts we shall be by next year. In any case, it's really something to be able to write in code. (1 October 1942)

Six months later, Anne wrote: *We have finished our Shorthand course; now we are beginning to practise speed, aren't we getting clever?* (27 March 1943)

Albert Dussel, whose real name was Fritz Pfeffer - he was also given a false name by Anne - fled to the Netherlands in 1938. The Frank family had known him for a few years. Anne had to share her room with him, and Margot went to sleep in her parents' bedroom.

This was the living-room and bedroom of Otto and Edith Frank. The door on the right opened into Anne's room. The curtains, which were always closed, are not shown on this photograph.
When Albert Dussel came, Margot also slept in this room on a camp bed which was set up every night.
The photograph was taken after the war. This room is also empty now.

Albert Dussel came a week later. He was amazed to find the Frank family. Like the neighbours, friends and acquaintances of the family, he had thought all that time that they had fled abroad.

Anne liked him, and listened to what Albert Dussel had to say about the outside world. It made everyone feel very sombre. *Countless friends and acquaintances have gone to a terrible end. Evening after evening the green and grey army lorries trundle past and ring at every front door to inquire if there are any Jews living in the house, if there are, then the whole family has to go at once. If they don't find any, they go on to the next house. No one has a chance of evading them, unless one goes into hiding. (...) Nobody is spared, old people, children, babies, expectant mothers, the sick, each and all join in the march of death.* (19 November 1942)

This made Anne realize how lucky she was in the Secret Annexe. She thought about her dearest friends who had been delivered into the hands of the cruellest brutes that walk the earth somewhere far away. And she lamented: *And all because they are Jews.* (19 November 1942)

The days and weeks crawled by. Autumn passed and winter came. It was cold and dark very early. After four o'clock or half past four, it was too dark to read.

We passed the time in all sorts of crazy ways: asking riddles, physical training in the dark, talking English and French, criticising books, but it all begins to pall in the end. (28 November 1942)

The families in hiding had now been living on top of each other for six months, always with the fear of being discovered. They could never go outside, not even for a little while.

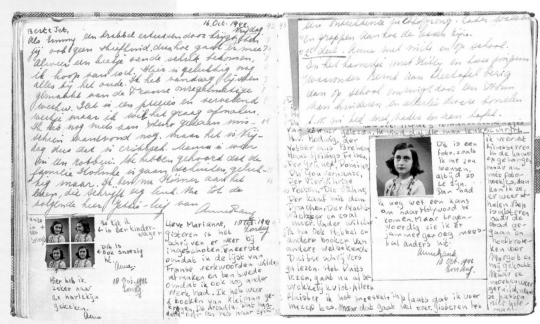

On 18 October 1942, Anne stuck a photograph of herself in her diary and wrote next to it: *This is a photo of me as I wish I looked all the time. Then I might still have a chance of getting to* Hollywood, but at present, I'm afraid I usually look quite different.

37

Anne stuck this photograph of Otto Frank in her diary.

Anne was very attached to her father. Otto defended her when the others criticised her, consoled her when she was sad, and helped her with her homework. He was her support and refuge. Otto understood how difficult it must be for the lively, active Anne to live in hiding. During the day, she had to whisper, and sit still as much as possible. And she could never, never go outside. Otto Frank tried to help her. Anne wrote: *(...) I adore Daddy, he is the one I look up to. I don't love anyone in the world but him.* (7 November 1942)

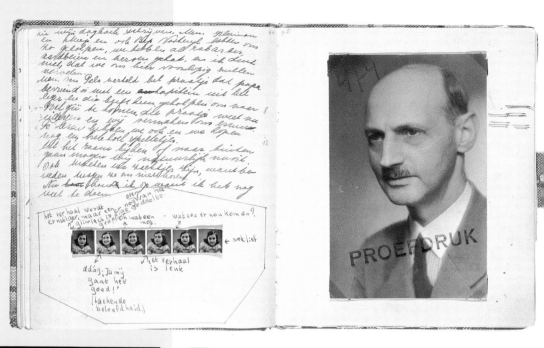

Anne's view of Albert Dussel changed. *Now he shows himself in his true colours; a stodgy, old-fashioned disciplinarian and preacher of long, drawn-out sermons on manners. As I have the unusual good fortune (!) to share my bedroom, alas, a small one, with his lordship and as I'm generally considered to be the most badly behaved of the three young people, I have a lot to put up with and have to sham deafness in order to escape the much too often repeated tickings-off and warnings.* (28 November 1942)

Nevertheless, the criticism of the others did not leave her unaffected. Anne only pretended. In reality, she often berated herself because she wanted to improve herself.

Now the trying part about me is that I criticize and scold myself far more than anyone else does. Then if Mummy adds her bit of advice the pile of sermons becomes so insurmountable that in my despair I become rude and start contradicting (...). (13 June 1944)

The new year, 1943, started. Every night the families heard hundreds of allied airplanes flying over. These planes were on their way to bomb German towns. This gave them hope. The opposition to Germany was getting stronger. Every evening they listened tensely to the English radio to hear the news about the war.

The allied planes flying over were shot at by the German anti-aircraft guns.

There were stores of food in the attic of the Secret Annexe. Sometimes the helpers succeeded in getting hold of large stocks of tins or beans on the black market. Miep and Bep went shopping every day. They used coupons* for their shopping. During the period that the families were in hiding, it became increasingly difficult to find enough food for them. In the Netherlands there was a shortage of food because the occupying forces took a great deal to Germany.

On 14 March 1944 Anne wrote: *Our food coupon suppliers have been caught so we just have our 5 black-market ration cards, and no coupons, and no fats. (...) Our supper today consists of a hash made from kale which has been preserved in a barrel. (...) It's incredible how kale that is probably a few years old can stink! The smell in the room is a mixture of bad plums, strong preservatives and 10 rotten eggs. Ugh! The mere thought of eating that muck makes me feel sick!*

I still haven't got over my fear of everything connected with shooting and planes, and I creep into Daddy's bed nearly every night for comfort. I know it's very childish but you don't know what it is like, the A.A. guns roar so loudly that you can't hear yourself speak. (10 March 1943)

Mrs. Van Daan was also very scared, but not only of the guns. One night she thought she heard a burglar in the attic, where the food was stored. No one took her seriously, but a few days later the noise woke the whole Van Daan family.

Peter went up to the attic with a torch and scamper, scamper, what do you think was running away? A swarm of enormous rats!

When we knew who the thieves were we let Mouschi sleep in the attic and the uninvited guests didn't come back again, at least (...) not during the night. (10 March 1943)

A few days later Peter went up to the attic to fetch some old newspapers. To get down the steps he had to hold the trapdoor firmly. Without looking, he put down his hand and ... almost fell down the steps with shock and pain. Without knowing it, he had put his hand on a large rat which bit him hard in his arm. The blood had soaked through his pyjamas when he came down with shaking knees, as white as a sheet. Anne could well imagine what it was like: *And no wonder; it's not very pleasant to stroke a large rat; and to get bitten into the bargain is really dreadful.* (10 March 1943)

Once the helpers were able to buy several bags of brown beans. Peter was asked to take the bags up to the attic.
He had managed to get 5 of the 6 sacks upstairs intact, and he was just busy pulling up number 6, when the bottom seam of the sack split, and a shower - no, a positive hailstorm of brown beans came pouring down and rattled down the stairs. There were about fifty pounds in the sack and the noise was enough to waken the dead. Downstairs they thought the old house with all its contents was coming down on them. It gave Peter a moment's fright, but he was soon roaring with laughter, especially when he saw me standing at the bottom of the stairs like a little island in the middle of a sea of beans! I was entirely surrounded up to my ankles in beans.* (9 November 1942)

School books
Every day Margot, Anne and Peter spent a few hours on their school subjects: languages, algebra, geometry, geography and history. They all hoped that the war would be over soon, and that they would be able to go back to school. Otto Frank was the one who helped them with their schoolwork. Anne wrote about it several times: *I have a great loathing for Algebra, Geometry and figures. I enjoy all the other school subjects, but history above all!* (6 April 1944)
Later she wrote: *(..) I've never loathed any other book so much as that one (...) If I'm ever in a very wicked mood I'll tear the blasted thing to pieces!* (20 May 1944)

Daily life

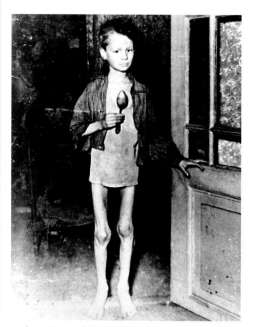

In the winter of 1944-1945, thousands of people died of hunger and cold in the west of the Netherlands.

At the beginning of the war most people tried not to interfere with anything. However, this became increasingly difficult as the war did interfere with them. Food became scarce, and coupons were issued. Chocolate, coffee, cigarettes and many other articles were virtually impossible to buy. People had to surrender their bicycles and radios. Anything of value was taken to Germany by the occupying forces. More and more people became very poor.

The newspapers only contained articles approved by the Germans. They announced that the German army was gaining victories everywhere, that members of the Resistance were criminals, and that Jews were inferior people.

More and more illegal* newspapers appeared. These newspapers were written and printed in secret. They said what was really happening. People also secretly listened to 'Radio Oranje'*. This was the daily broadcast in Dutch on the English wavelength.

In 1943, it was becoming clear that Germany would lose the war. People increasingly complained openly. The Resistance gained strength, but the German occupying forces tried to suppress the Resistance. Members of the Resistance were often simply shot dead in

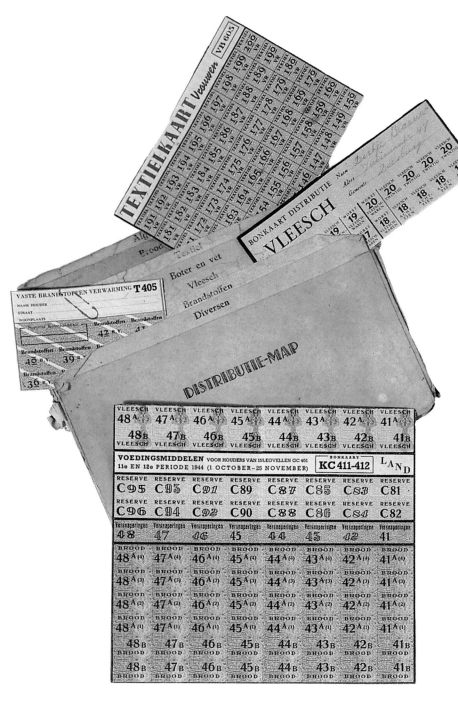

the street. In this way the Germans tried to intimidate people.

In the autumn of 1944, the Allies liberated the south of the Netherlands. The rest of the Netherlands remained occupied. That winter there was a severe lack of food in the west of the Netherlands. In the big cities particularly, there was hardly any food left. About 20,000 people died that winter from hunger, cold and disease.

On 5 May 1945, the whole of the Netherlands was liberated after five years of war.

As food was scarce, coupons were issued. Everyone received a certain quantity. If people wished to buy something, they had to surrender a coupon as well as paying money. In this way everything was shared as fairly as possible. People who were in hiding did not have an official address, and were therefore not issued any coupons.

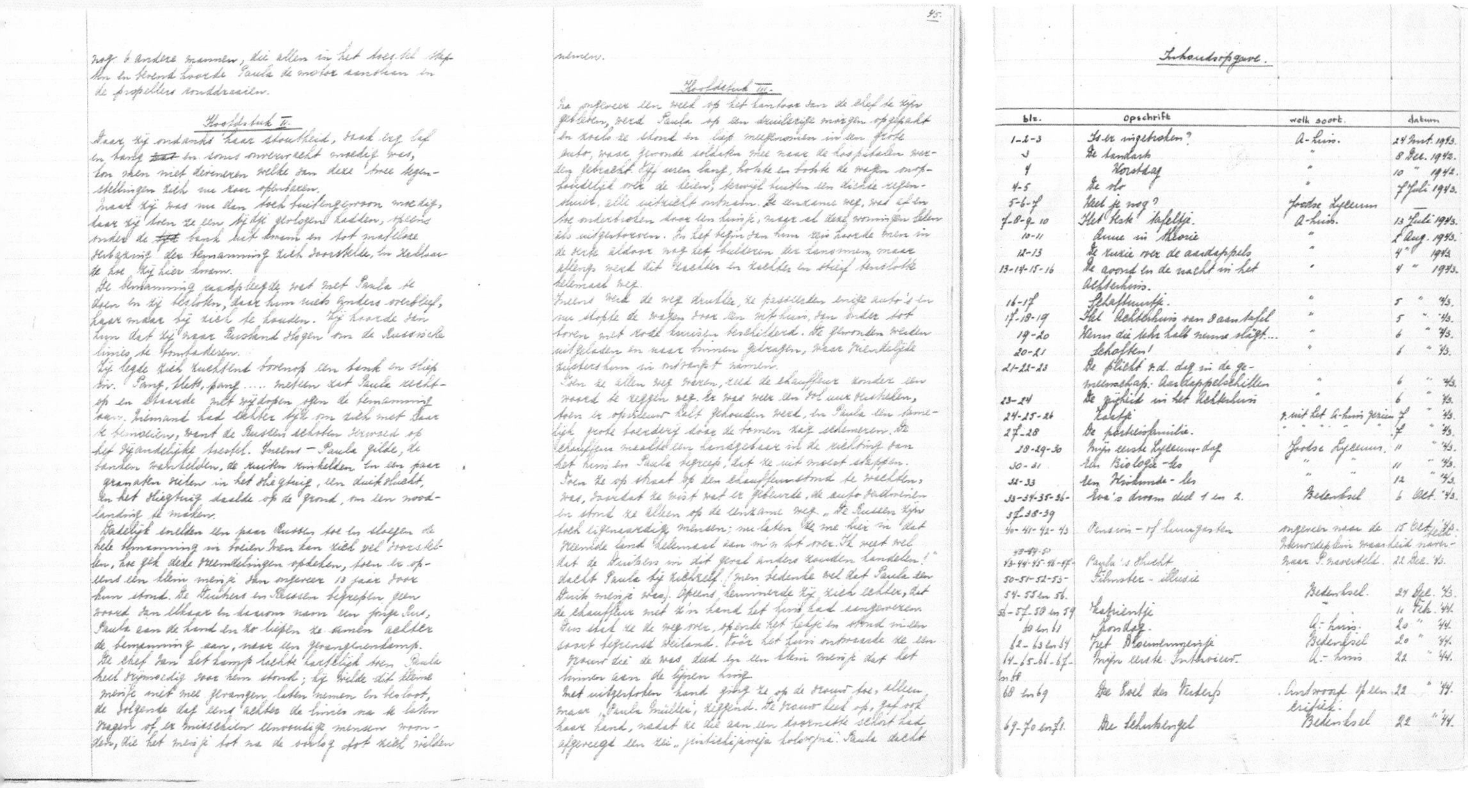

Anne enjoyed writing very much. She didn't just write in her diary. In 1943, she also started writing a story book. This was entitled: 'Stories and events from the Secret Annexe.' In these stories she described things which had happened in the Secret Annexe, and memories from her schooldays. She also wrote imaginary stories, including fairy tales, which she called 'made-up stories'.

The thing you notice straightaway about the story book is that it looks very tidy. Anne covered page after page in neat writing with her fountain pen. She hardly crossed anything out or made any mistakes. The chapters were carefully divided up, and in this way it was just like a real book. By way of introduction to the story 'Paula's flight', she started: *Long ago, when I was little, Papa used to tell me stories about 'naughty Paula'; he had a whole collection of stories and I was crazy about them. And now again, when I'm with Papa at night, he sometimes tells me about Paula, and I've written down the latest story.* (22 December 1943)

Spring 1943. The families in hiding were tense and tired. Everyone was suffering from lack of sleep because of the airplanes and the anti-aircraft fire. The food they were eating was poor. There were shortages of everything. Miep and Bep had more and more trouble finding things to eat. Anne greatly admired the Dutch people who were helping those in hiding, for it was difficult and dangerous work.

(...) it is amazing how much noble, unselfish work these people are doing, risking their own lives to help and save others. Our helpers are a very good example. (...) Never have we heard one word of the burden which we certainly must be to them, never has one of them complained of all the trouble we give. (28 January 1944)

Anne often realized that she should not complain. *If I just think of how we live here, I usually come to the conclusion that it is a paradise compared with how other Jews who are not in hiding must be living* (2 May 1943)

On Friday morning, 16 July 1943, the people in hiding were shocked when they noticed that a burglar had been in the warehouse. Both the door of the warehouse and the front door were open. The doors had been forced with a crowbar. Johannes Kleiman, who arrived at the office a little later, discovered that two cashboxes had been stolen. But worst of all, the thieves had also taken coupons for 150 kilos of sugar. Everyone was scared that the burglars had noticed there was someone hiding upstairs and would betray them to the police....

But fortunately days went by and nothing happened.

1942 - 1944

The families tried to live life as normally as possible, and they had a fixed schedule for every day. But the days were so long. Would the war go on for much longer? How long would they all keep it up? These were the questions they all asked themselves.

But on 8 September 1943, there was new hope of a happy ending. On the radio they heard that Italy, an ally of Germany, had surrendered to the Allies. Would the war end in 1943 after all...?

But events did not move that fast, and the Allied Invasion*, which they hoped for every day, did not take place. In the autumn of 1943, Anne was frequently in a very gloomy mood.

My nerves often get the better of me: it is especially on Sundays that I feel rotten. The atmosphere is so oppressive, and sleepy and as heavy as lead; you don't hear a single bird singing outside, and a deadly sultry silence hangs everywhere, catching hold of me as if it would drag me down deep into an underworld. (...) 'Go outside, laugh, and take a breath of fresh air', a voice cries within me; but I don't even feel a response any more; I go and lie on the divan and sleep, to make the time pass more quickly, and the stillness and the terrible fear, because there is no way of killing time. (29 October 1943)

Anne was just thirteen when she went into hiding. She was growing visibly. On the wall in Mr. and Mrs. Frank's room, just next to the door to Anne's room, they kept a record of Anne and Margot's heights. The stripes on the wall show that during her time in the Secret Annexe, Anne grew a full thirteen centimetres. The fact that Anne was growing so much led to problems. All the clothes which she had brought with her in July 1942 became much too small. Sometimes Miep or Bep would bring her something new. *Mummy and Margot have managed the whole winter with 3 vests between them, and mine are so small that they don't even come to my tummy.* (2 May 1943)

Sometimes when there was no one in the office, they would leave their hiding place for a bit. When it was dark, Anne would look out of the office window at the front of the house. From behind the curtain, she would see people passing by. In this way, she caught a glimpse of the outside world. Of course, they made very sure that they could not be seen.

42

The diary which Anne received for her thirteenth birthday in 1942 had been filled up a long time before. After that she kept her diary in exercise books and cashbooks which Miep and Bep gave her. In January 1944, Anne re-read her 'old' diary, and realized that in the previous year and a half she had changed a great deal. She thought she had become much 'wiser'. When she noticed that there were still two empty pages, Anne wrote down her thoughts about what she had read. *When I look over my diary today, 1,5 years on, I cannot believe that I was ever such an innocent young thing. (...) I still understand those moods, those remarks about Margot, Mummy and Daddy so well that I might have written them yesterday, but I no longer understand how I could write so freely about other things. (22 January 1944)*

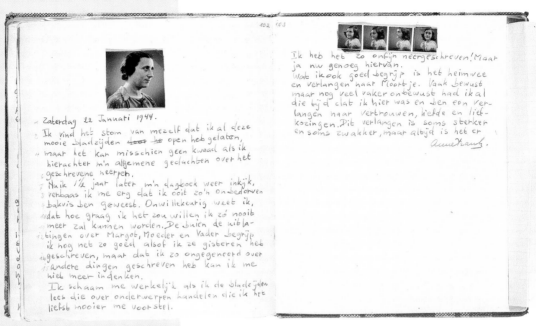

Wednesday, 23 February 1944
Dear Kitty,
It's lovely weather outside and I've quite perked up since yesterday. Nearly every morning I go to the attic to blow the stuffy air out of my lungs; (...) this morning when I went up to the attic again, Peter was busy clearing up. He was finished very quickly and when I sat down on my favourite spot on the floor, he joined me. Both of us looked at the glorious blue of the sky, the bare chestnut tree on whose branches little raindrops shone, at the seagulls and other birds that looked like silver in the sun. (...) He stood with his head against a thick beam, and I sat down. We breathed the fresh air, looked outside, and both felt that the spell should not be broken by words.

It was 1944. Anne was now more than fourteen and a half years old. The group of eight people had been hiding in the Secret Annexe for a year and a half. Anne noticed that she was changing, and she wrote about this in her diary. She spent much more time thinking about all sorts of things, and also viewed the people she was hiding with in a new light. Anne also noticed that she was changing physically.

I think what is happening to me is so wonderful, and not only what can be seen on my body, but all that is taking place inside. I never discuss myself or any of these things with anybody; that is why I have to talk to myself about them. (5 January 1944)

Anne was no longer a noisy schoolgirl. She was growing up and... fell in love !

Anne fell in love with Peter. She wanted to talk to him about everything that was on her mind. But Peter was shy and avoided her. However, Anne found a way of getting to talk to him.

I tried to think of an excuse to stay unobtrusively in his room and get him talking, and my chance came yesterday. Peter has a mania for crossword puzzles at the moment (...) we soon sat opposite each other at his little table, he on the chair and me on the divan.

It gave me a queer feeling when I looked into his deep blue eyes and saw how embarrassed this unexpected visit had made him. (...) I noticed his shy manner and it made me feel very gentle. (6 January 1944)

In the following weeks Anne and Peter became more and more familiar with each other, although Peter was still shy. Anne often went to Peter's room and they talked about all sorts of things.

She thought a great deal about her life up to that time and about the future. She thought back to the happy, carefree days before they had to go into hiding. Going into hiding had changed everything. She had changed herself as well. She had become rebellious and insolent and was constantly told off by the adults around her. Now, a year and a half later, she thought that she was much 'wiser'. She was still sometimes cheerful and boisterous, and always had something to say about everyone. But according to Anne, that was only the superficial exterior, the only side which other people saw of her. She thought she had changed 'inside'. Anne had become aware of her good and bad qualities and of the things she thought were important in life. She wanted to be happy. She did not want to think about all the misery in the world, but about all the beautiful things that remained. It bothered her very much that the adults still treated her so often like a child. *Although I am only fourteen, I know quite well what I want, I know who is right and who is wrong, I have my opinions, my own ideas and principles (...).* (17 March 1944)

On 12 January 1944, Anne wrote about Margot. *Margot has grown so sweet; she seems quite different from what she used to be, isn't nearly so catty these days and is becoming a real friend. Nor does she any longer regard me as a little kid who counts for nothing.*

For a time Anne thought that Margot was also in love with Peter, but that was not the case. However, Margot was a little bit jealous. In a letter to Anne, she wrote: *I only feel a bit sorry that I haven't found anyone yet, and am not likely to for the time being, with whom I can discuss my thoughts and feelings.* (20 March 1944)

Anne and Margot wrote letters to each other, for as Anne wrote: *(...) Because I can say what I mean much better on paper.* (8 March 1944)

Anne was very critical of her mother. She thought her mother did not understand her or take her seriously. They often quarrelled, but Anne kept trying to make it up. On 2 March 1944, Anne described one of these quarrels. Bep was with them in the Secret Annexe and was helping with the washing up. She was talking to Edith Frank and Mrs. Van Daan about feeling discouraged. Anne was listening to the conversation. *Do you know what her advice was? She should try to think of all the other people who are in trouble! What is the good of thinking about misery when one is already miserable oneself? I said this too and was naturally told to keep out of this sort of conversation!* (2 March 1944)

Anne was furious. *Aren't the grown-ups idiotic and stupid? (...) I'm not allowed to open my mouth! (...) We aren't even allowed to have any opinions!* (2 March 1944)

The warehouse
While the Franks were in hiding, there were at least three burglaries. More and more people were stealing, because of the increasing shortages of everything in Amsterdam. Each time, the family was afraid that the thieves had noticed something and would betray them. But there was another danger. Two of the members of staff who worked in the warehouse had not been told about the hiding place. At least one of them suspected something, and was curious. He knew there had once been an entrance to the Secret Annexe, and regularly saw Miep and Bep go upstairs with lots of shopping.

Anne often visited Peter in the attic. This made her both happy and unhappy at the same time: *When Peter and I are sitting somewhere together, on a hard, wooden crate in the midst of masses of rubbish and dust, our arms around each other's shoulders, and very close; he with one of my curls in his hand. When the birds sing outside and you see the trees changing to green, the sun invites one to be out in the open air, when the sky is so blue, then - oh, then I wish for so much!* (14 April 1944)

On Saturday evening 18 March, Anne visited Peter again. *He was standing on the left side of the open window; I went and stood on the right side, and we talked. It was much easier to talk beside the open window in semi-darkness than in bright light and I believe Peter felt the same. We told each other so much, so very very much, that I can't repeat it all, but it was lovely, the most wonderful evening I have ever had in the Secret Annexe.* (19 March 1944)

The adults were very curious about what Peter and Anne were discussing together. They made silly jokes about it, and Anne's parents were also rather worried about their daughter.

On Saturday evening 9 April 1944 there was yet another burglary. Not the first burglary, but this time it was more frightening than ever. The front door onto the street had been destroyed, and it seemed as if someone had warned the police. The police came to search the building

Then, a quarter past 11, a bustle and noise downstairs. Everyone's breath was audible, in other respects no one moved. Footsteps in the house, in the private office, kitchen, then.... on our staircase, no one breathed audibly now, 8 hearts thumped, footsteps on our staircase, than a rattling of the swinging cupboard. This moment is indescribable: 'Now we are lost!' I said, and could see all fifteen of us being carried off by the Gestapo that very night. (11 April 1944)

1942 - 1944

On Wednesday, 29 March 1944, during the daily radio broadcast from London, Anne heard the Dutch minister, Bolkestein. He said that after the war all the diaries and letters about the war would be collected. Anne fantasized: *Just imagine how interesting it would be if I were to publish a romance of the Secret Annexe.* (29 March 1944) She could not forget the idea. A week later she wrote: *(...) Will I ever become a journalist or a writer? I hope so, oh, I hope so very much, for I can recapture everything when I write, my thoughts, my ideals and my fantasies.* (5 April 1944)
On 11 May 1944, she confided in her diary: *(...) You've known for a long time that my greatest wish is to become a journalist some day and later on a famous writer (...) In any case, I want to publish a book entitled, 'Het Achterhuis' after the war. Whether I shall succeed or not, I cannot say, but my diary will be a great help.*

Twice they rattled the cupboard, then a tin can fell down, the footsteps withdrew, we were saved thus far! A shiver seemed to pass from one to the other. I heard someone's teeth chattering, no one said a word (...). (11 April 1944)

They all spent the night together in the Van Daan's room. No one slept. They were all terrified. The next morning they were delighted when the helpers called in. Once again, everything had ended happily.

15 April 1944 was an important day in Anne's life. She received her first kiss. Peter and Anne were sitting close together on the divan in Peter's room.

How I suddenly made the right move, I don't know, but before we went downstairs he kissed me, through my hair, half on my left cheek, half on my ear; I tore downstairs without looking round, and am simply longing for today. (16 April 1944)

In the following days she thought a great deal about that first kiss and how things would go on now.

In her diary she wrote: *Dear Kitty, Do you think that Daddy and Mummy would approve of my sitting and kissing a boy on a divan - a boy of seventeen and a half and a girl of just under fifteen? I don't really think they would, but I must rely on myself over this. It is so quiet and peaceful to lie in his arms and to dream, it is so thrilling to feel his cheek against mine, it is so lovely to know that there is someone waiting for me.* (17 April 1944)

The sheets of paper of Anne's diary and her photograph album. When Anne had filled her first diary, she continued writing in exercise books and cashbooks. She kept everything in a leather briefcase which had belonged to her father. A few weeks after the radio broadcast, she decided to rewrite her diary so that it could be published after the war. Sometimes she left out pieces from her original diary, and sometimes she made some additions. She copied everything onto thin sheets of tracing paper which came from the office. Sometimes she doubted the point of doing all this. On 14 April 1944, she wrote: *I really believe, Kits, that I'm slightly bats today, and yet I don't know why. Everything here is so mixed up, nothing's connected any more, and sometimes I very much doubt whether in the future anyone will be interested in all my tosh. 'The unbosomings of an ugly duckling' will be the title of all this nonsense.*

Anne wrote a long letter to her father to explain why she would continue to visit Peter. At the end of it she wrote: *You can't and mustn't regard me as fourteen, for all these troubles have made me older; I shall not be sorry for what I have done but shall act as I think I can!* (5 May 1944) She asked Otto to trust her through thick and thin, but her father was angry and disappointed. Later Anne was sorry about her angry and passionate letter, but not about her feelings for Peter. *I am not alone any more; he loves me, I love him. (...)* (7 May 1944)

This is the map that Otto Frank pinned on the wall of the room. He indicated the advance of the Allied Forces in France with coloured pins. Every day for more than a year they had all hoped for the invasion. At last it was happening.
Could we be granted victory this year, this 1944? We don't know yet, but hope lives on; it gives us fresh courage, and makes us strong again. Since we must put up bravely with all the fears, privations, and sufferings, the great thing now is to remain calm and steadfast, now we must clench our teeth rather than cry out! (...) Oh Kitty, the best part of the invasion is that I have the feeling that friends are approaching. (6 June 1944)

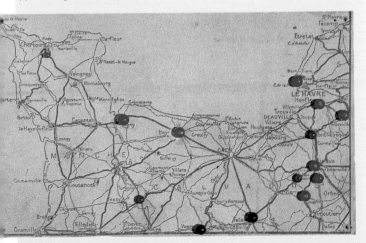

Anne decided to talk to her father about it. When they were alone one day, she asked: *'Daddy I expect you've gathered that when we are together, Peter and I don't sit miles apart. Do you think it's wrong?'* (2 May 1944)

Her father warned Anne that she should be careful. The next day he told her that it would be better if she did not go to Peter's room so often. But Anne did not want to obey her father.

(...) Not only because I like being with Peter; but I have told him that I trust him, I do trust him and I want to show him that I do, which can't happen if I stay downstairs through lack of trust. No, I'm going. (2 May 1944)

In the spring of 1944, Anne also wrote about other things than being in love. The everlasting war was always on her mind. *(...) What, oh, what is the use of the war, why can't people live peacefully together, why all this destruction? (...) Oh why are people so crazy?* (3 May 1944)

But Anne also wrote: *I am young and I possess many buried qualities (...) I have been given a lot, a happy nature, a great deal of cheerfulness and strength. Every day I feel that I am developing inwardly, that the liberation is drawing nearer and how beautiful nature is, how good the people about me, how interesting and amusing this adventure! Why, then, should I be in despair?* (3 May 1944)

On 6 June 1944, the news of the Normandy invasion in France was on the radio! Anne was ecstatic. *Great commotion in the Secret Annexe. Would the long-awaited liberation, about which so much has been said, but which still seems too wonderful, too much like a fairy tale, ever come true.* (6 June 1944)

Anne celebrated her fifteenth birthday six days after the invasion on 12 June. They had been in the Secret Annexe for almost two years. For the time being the liberation was still a long way away, and life on the Prinsengracht went on.

Anne was disappointed in Peter. She had hoped for a good friend with whom she could talk about everything, but that still wasn't really happening. She wondered whether he might simply be superficial or whether he was still shy. She didn't know, but she understood that the whole situation was difficult for Peter as well. Anne thought these times were much more difficult for young people than for older people. Older people are so sure about everything; they have far fewer doubts. *It's twice as hard for us young ones to hold our ground, and maintain our opinions, in a time when all ideals are being shattered and destroyed, when people are showing their worst side, and do not know whether to believe in truth and right and in God. (...) That's the difficulty in these times, ideals, dreams and cherished hopes rise within us, only to meet the horrible truth and be shattered. It's really a wonder that I haven't dropped all my ideals, because they seem so absurd and impossible to carry out. Yet I keep them, because in spite of everything I still believe that people are really good at heart.* (15 July 1944)

The helpers, including Miep (on the left) and Bep, knew that they were risking their lives by helping their friends to hide. Anne was very aware of the danger they were in. On 26 May 1944, Anne wrote: *Miep and Kugler carry the heaviest burden of us and all those in hiding, Miep in all she does, and Kugler through the enormous responsibility for the 8 of us, which is sometimes so much for him that he can hardly talk from pent-up nerves and strain.*

This is the last time that Anne wrote in her diary.
On Tuesday, 1 August 1944, Anne wrote that she thought it was a shame that the others in the Secret Annexe only really knew one side of her. She was often berated and criticized for that side, and that is why the others did not take her seriously. *I have already told you before that I have, as it were, a dual personality. One half embodies my exuberant cheerfulness, making fun of everything, vivacity, and above all the way I take everything lightly. (...) This side is usually lying in wait and pushes away the other, which is much better, deeper and purer. (...) no one knows Anne's better side.*
Three days later the German police entered the Secret Annexe.

The Westertoren seen from the attic window of the Secret Annexe.

I simply can't build up my hopes on a foundation consisting of confusion, misery, and death. I see the world gradually being turned into a wilderness, I hear the ever-approaching thunder, which will destroy us too, I can feel the sufferings of millions and yet, if I look up into the heavens, I think that it will all come right, that this cruelty too will end, and that peace and tranquillity will return again. In the meantime, I must uphold my ideals, for perhaps the time will come when I shall be able to carry them out! (15 July 1944)

On 21 July 1944 Anne was happy and optimistic. The news about the war seemed hopeful for a happy ending. She made one more entry in her diary.

On 4 August between ten o' clock and half past ten in the morning the German police stormed the Secret Annexe. They had been betrayed....

The diary was left behind

The policeman who arrested the families was called Karl Silberbauer.

It was a beautiful hot summer's day. As usual, Otto Frank went to Peter's room in the morning to give him an English lesson. It was a day like any other. Mr. Frank looked at his watch. It was almost half past ten. He wanted to start teaching.

At that moment Peter raised his hand. He looked frightened. From downstairs they heard noises, strange men's voices, shouting, threatening voices...

A few minutes earlier, five men had suddenly entered the office building. One of them was wearing the uniform of the German police. The others were in civilian clothes. They were probably Dutch Nazis. Miep, Bep, Johannes Kleiman, and Victor Kugler were in the office.

The men knew everything. Victor Kugler had to go with them. They went upstairs. The men drew their revolvers when they got to the bookcase. They opened the cupboard and went inside.

A minute later one of the Dutch Nazis went into Peter's room, pointing his revolver at him. Otto and Peter went downstairs. They saw all the others, including Anne and Margot, with their hands up. Karl Silberbauer, the policeman, barked out an abrupt demand for money and jewellery. He grabbed a briefcase and emptied it onto the floor. It was the papers from Anne's diaries. He put the money and jewellery into the briefcase. Karl Silberbauer did not believe that they had all been hiding in the Secret Annexe for more than two years. Then Otto Frank showed him the marks on the wall, where Anne's height had been measured.

Johannes Kleiman next to the bookcase, after the war.

On 4 August 1944, the eight people who had been hiding in the Secret Annexe were taken to the German police station in a covered lorry. It was located in two schools which the Germans had commandeered. The day after their arrest they were transferred to another building and put in a cell there.

Miep Gies did not just take the papers of Anne's diary from the Secret Annexe. She also took the photo albums of the Frank family and a number of school books.

The Germans emptied the houses of Jews who had been taken away. All the contents were taken, and anything of value went to Germany. The company which did this for the Germans was the Puls company. This is why the people of Amsterdam referred to 'pulsing' a house.

They were allowed to pack a few clothes. Then they were taken in a lorry to a German police station. Victor Kugler and Johannes Kleiman were also arrested and taken away. Later they were interned in a camp. They both survived.

After that it was quiet on the Prinsengracht. Miep and Bep had not been taken away. They were afraid that the men would come back to arrest them at any moment. At the end of the afternoon they went upstairs together with Jan Gies and Van Maaren, the storeman. They went into the Secret Annexe. There was chaos everywhere. They saw the pages of Anne's diary on the floor and took them downstairs with other papers and books. These also included the photo albums of the Frank family. Miep put the pages of the diary in her desk drawer and locked it. About a week later the whole Secret Annexe was emptied on German orders.

It has always remained a mystery who betrayed the hiding place to the Germans.

The family spent four days locked in a cell. Then, on 8 August they were transferred to the Westerbork camp. They stayed there for the whole of the month of August in the so-called 'punishment barracks'. They were 'punishable prisoners' because they had not given themselves up, but had been rounded up while they were in hiding.

Westerbork was an overcrowded camp. Every week a goods train left for one of the extermination camps* with more than a thousand men, women and children. The eight people from the Secret Annexe were on the last train which went from Westerbork to Auschwitz.

51

After 1944

On 3 September 1944, they were put on the last train transporting prisoners to the Auschwitz concentration camp in Poland, together with more than a thousand other people. They were cooped up in a goods wagon, together with about seventy other people for three days, and arrived in Auschwitz on the night of 5 September. More than half of the people were gassed that very day, including nearly all the children under fifteen. Anne was spared because she had just had her fifteenth birthday. The men were separated from the women, and most never saw each other again. The women had to walk to the women's camp in Birkenau. Edith Frank and her two daughters stayed together. Mrs. Van Pels (Van Daan) also went to that women's camp.

Otto Frank, Peter van Pels (Van Daan), and Fritz Pfeffer (Albert Dussel), went to the men's camp.

The conditions in Auschwitz were terrible. The prisoners were given hardly anything to eat. Every day large numbers of people died from starvation and illness. There were no medicines. Every day the guards would beat or club people to death for no reason at all, and every day new groups of prisoners were gassed. No one could be sure of their life. Every day could be their last.

Hermann van Pels was murdered in the gas chambers of Auschwitz a couple of weeks later. Fritz Pfeffer ended up in the Neuengamme concentration camp. He died there on 20 December 1944.

The Russian armies approached from the east and the Allies were coming from the west. The Germans knew that they had lost the war. They wanted to wipe out the traces of their crimes as far as possible. Many of the camps were cleared and dismantled.

In some cases they shot the prisoners and buried them in mass graves. Many prisoners were also transferred to other concentration camps which were further away from the front.

The platform at Auschwitz-Birkenau. This is where the families from the Secret Annexe arrived, and where the selection took place. People who were strong enough to work for the Germans were allowed to live (a little longer). The others, including children under fifteen, in most cases went straight to the gas chambers. Anne escaped this because she had just had her fifteenth birthday.

The list of names of people who were on the last transport from Westerbork to Auschwitz include the names of the Frank family.

5	Judentransport aus den Niederlanden — Lager Westerbork			Blatt 7
	3.September			
	am Häftlinge		194 .	
301. Engers	Isidor	30.4. 93	Kaufmann
302. Engers	Leonard	13.6. 20	Landarbeiter
303. Franco	Manfred	1.5. 05	Verleger
304. Frank	Arthur	22.8. 81	Kaufmann
305. Frank	Isaac	29.11.87	Installateur
306. Frank	Margot	16.2. 26	ohne
307. Frank	Otto	12.5. 89	Kaufmann
308. Frank-Hollaender	Edith	16.1. 00	ohne
309. Frank	Anneliese	12.6. 29	ohne
310. v.Franck	Sara	27.4. 02	Typistin
311. Franken	Abraham	16.5. 96	Landarbeiter
312. Franken-Weyand	Johanna	24.12.96	Landbauer
313. Franken	Hermann	12.5. 34	ohne
314. Franken	Louis	10.8. 17	Gaertner
315. Franken	Rosalina	29.3. 27	Landbau
316. Frankfort	Alex	14.11.19	Dr.i.d.Oekonomie
317. Frankfort-Elzas	Regina	11.12.19	Apoth.-Ass.
318. Frankfoort	Elias	22.10.98	Schneider
319. Frankfort	Max	20.8. 21	Schneider
320. Frankfort-Weijl	Hetty	25.3. 24	Näherin
321. Frankfort-Berkendam	Rozette	24.6. 98	Schriftstellerin
322. Frijda	Herman	22.6. 87	Hochschullehrer
323. Frank	Henriette	28.4. 21	Typistin

The murder of millions of people

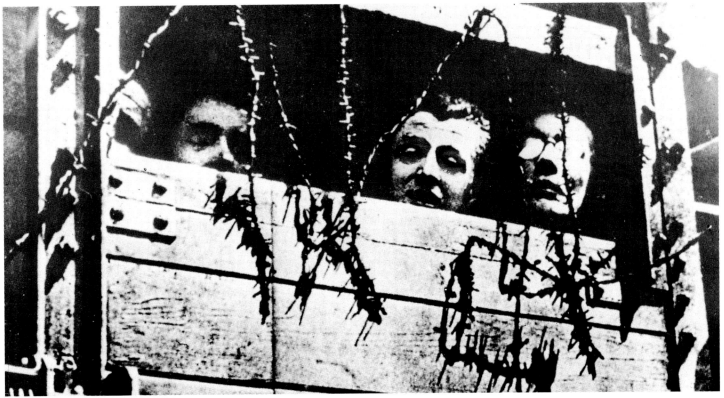

People were packed together in cattle wagons for days on end before the trains arrived at the camps.

These are gypsy children from a German children's home. Shortly after this photograph was taken, they were transported to Auschwitz and murdered.

The Nazis declared that the German people were a sort of super race. They thought that in their empire there was no place for people they considered inferior, such as gypsies, blacks, handicapped people and Jews.

In January 1942, the leadership of the Nazi party decided to murder more than eleven million European Jews. Simply because they were Jews. For this purpose they built extermination camps. These were concentration camps specially designed for the rapid execution of people. These camps were built in isolated areas in Poland, in Auschwitz-Birkenau, Treblinka, Belzec, Sobibor, Chelmno and Majdanek. This was done in total secrecy. No one was to know the real reason why the Jews were deported. This is why the Nazis said that the Jews were taken to Poland to work. Most people believed this.

Trains from all the European countries occupied by the Germans went backwards and forwards to Poland. The Jews were crowded together in cattle trucks for days on end with nothing to eat or drink, not knowing what was to become of them. Most people were taken straight to the extermination camps. Auschwitz-Birkenau was the largest of these camps. Most people were murdered in the gas chambers a few hours after arriving. The Nazis spared for a while only those people they thought they could use. Strong young men and women had to work incredibly hard for the Germans. The conditions were so terrible that most died within a few weeks. A few very lucky ones were still alive when the Allied Forces liberated the camps in 1945. Altogether about six million Jews had been murdered. The gypsies had also been deported to the camps from all the countries occupied by the Germans. The great majority did not survive the war.

After 1944

When Anne, Margot and their mother arrived in Auschwitz-Birkenau, there were about 39,000 women in the camp. Their hair was shaved and a number was tattooed on their arms.

For the last few months before the liberation in April 1945, the camp in Bergen-Belsen was extremely over-crowded. Most of the inmates were women. They were crowded together in barracks. Contagious diseases raged. Anne and Margot also fell ill. These photographs of Bergen-Belsen were taken just after the liberation.

Anne and Margot had to leave their mother behind at the end of October 1944. Like Mrs. Van Pels, the two girls were transferred to the concentration camp at Bergen-Belsen.

There too, the conditions were indescribable. It was icy cold and there was hardly anything to eat. The camp was overcrowded and contagious diseases raged.

Edith Frank survived in Auschwitz for another two months. She died on 6 January 1945.

Like most other prisoners, Peter van Pels was taken from Auschwitz by the SS guards* on 16 January. This was ten days before the Russian army liberated Auschwitz. He died in the Mauthausen camp in Austria on 5 May 1945. Mrs. Van Pels was in Bergen-Belsen only for a short while. She then went to Theresienstadt via Buchenwald. She died there in the spring of 1945.

Margot and Anne tried to survive in Bergen-Belsen. They slept in an overcrowded, unheated barracks with a large number of other women. Some women who survived the camp saw Anne and Margot there and talked to them.

'I saw Anne and her sister again in the barracks. (…) The Frank girls were almost unrecognizable since their hair had been cut off. (…) And they were cold.' (Mrs. Van Amerongen-Frankfoorder)

The conditions in Bergen-Belsen were so bad that scores of thousands of people died. Anne and Margot died a few weeks before the camp was liberated by the English.

Anne's schoolfriend ('Lies') turned out to be in another part of the camp. She talked to Anne through the barbed wire. '(…) it was so terrible. She immediately began to cry, and she told me, "I don't have any parents anymore". (…) I always think, if Anne had known that her father was still alive, she might have had more strength to survive (…).' (Mrs. Pick-Goslar)

Another woman related: '(…) she told me that she had such a horror of the lice and fleas in her clothes and that she had thrown all of her clothes away. It was the middle of winter and she was wrapped in one blanket.'
(Mrs. Brandes-Brilleslijper)

'The Frank girls were so emaciated. They looked terrible. (…) it was clear that they had typhus. You could really see both of them dying.'
(Mrs. Van Amerongen-Frankfoorder)

Margot died one day in March 1945. A few days later, Anne died as well. The camp was liberated by English soldiers a few weeks later in April.

Otto Frank was the only one from the Secret Annexe to survive the war. He was still in Auschwitz when the Russians liberated the camp on 27 January 1945. He wanted to go back to Amsterdam, but the war had not ended in the Netherlands. Otto started the long journey home to Amsterdam on 5 March 1945. The Russians took him, together with the others, to the port of Odessa on the Black Sea coast. From Odessa, he went by boat to Marseilles in France, and from there, by train and lorry to Amsterdam.

The Allied Forces liberated the remaining Jews in the concentration camps in Germany and Poland. The soldiers could hardly believe their eyes. The difficult journey home started for the survivors. Most had lost all their family and friends. Often their stories were not believed, or no one was interested. Only 4,700 Jews returned to the Netherlands from the camps.

After 1944

Otto Frank went to live with Miep and Jan Gies. This photograph was taken in 1951. In 1952 he moved to Basel. A year later he married Elfriede Geiringer.

The Dutch Red Cross did not issue an official declaration until 1954. This confirmed that Anne Frank had died in Bergen-Belsen in 1945. There was also a declaration about Margot.

■ Otto Frank did not arrive in Amsterdam until 3 June, and immediately went to see Miep and Jan Gies.

Their reunion was full of joy and sadness. Otto Frank said that he had heard that his wife Edith was dead, but he still hoped that Anne and Margot were alive. He had heard that they had been taken to Bergen-Belsen, and that at least Bergen-Belsen was not an extermination camp. Otto moved in with Miep and Jan. Every day they tried to get news about Anne and Margot.

Almost two months later Otto received news that both his daughters had died.

All this time Miep had kept Anne's diaries to give them back to Anne herself. As it was now certain that Anne was dead, Miep got out the diaries and gave them to Otto. Otto started reading them straightaway and was moved and astonished. He had never realized that Anne had recorded everything that happened in the Secret Annexe so well and so accurately.

Otto typed large chunks of the diary in German, and sent them to his mother in Switzerland.

Later he also let other people read parts of the diary. Other people urged him to look for a publisher, but straight after the war, no one wanted to start on this. It was only when an article appeared on Anne's diaries in the newspaper 'Het Parool' on 3 April 1946, that a publisher was found. Anne Frank's diary was published in an edition of 1,500 copies in the summer of 1947.

In this way, Otto fulfilled Anne's wish to become a writer.

Like many of the Jews who returned, Otto Frank placed a notice in the newspaper in the 'Information requested about' column. On 1 August 1945, this entry read: 'MARGOT FRANK (19) and ANNA FRANK (16) in Jan. on trans. from Bergen-Belsen. O. Frank, Prinsengracht 263, tel. 37059'.

Otto Frank in 1967.
Otto died in Birsfelden, a suburb of Basel, on 30 August 1980 at the age of 91. He donated the pages of Anne's diary to the State of the Netherlands.

The book was soon translated into French. Then it was translated into German, and in 1951, an English edition was published. In the years that followed it was translated into thirty-one other languages.

The diary became world famous. Now, more than forty-five years later, the book has been published in fifty-five languages, more than twenty million copies have been sold, and plays and films have been made about it. Throughout the world, streets and schools have been named after Anne Frank.

For many people Anne Frank became the symbol of the six million Jews who were murdered by the Nazis in the Second World War. It is almost impossible to imagine this number, but the story of Anne Frank makes it possible to get some idea of what it meant for each of those six million men, women and children.

Otto Frank spent the rest of his life spreading Anne's ideas and ideals. In 1979, one year before his death, he wrote:

'Anne never spoke about hatred anywhere in her diary. She wrote that despite everything, she believed in the goodness of people. And that when the war was over, she wanted to work for the world and for people. This is the duty I have taken over from her. I have received many thousands of letters. Young people especially always want to know how these terrible things could ever have happened. I answer them as well as I can, and I often finish by saying: "I hope that Anne's book will have an effect on the rest of your life so that insofar as it is possible in your circumstances, you will work for unity and peace".'

On 3 April 1946, an article entitled 'The voice of a child' appeared in the newspaper 'Het Parool'. In his article Professor J. Romein wrote about Anne's diary: 'By coincidence I came across a diary that was written during the war. The Netherlands State Institute for War Documentation already has about 200 of such diaries, but it would surprise me if there was one other which was as pure, as intelligent and yet as human as this one. (...)'

Some examples of editions of The Diary of Anne Frank in different languages.

The Anne Frank House

You've known for a long time that my greatest wish is to become (...) a famous writer. (Anne Frank, 11 May 1944)

Anne Frank's wish was fulfilled after her death. She is now a famous writer. People throughout the world have read her diary. Because she was able to describe so well what happened to her, Anne Frank has become a symbol of the fate of millions of Jews in the Second World War. But also for all the people who are persecuted now for their background, the colour of their skin, or their beliefs.

After the war, the house where the Frank family had gone into hiding, Prinsengracht 263 in Amsterdam, continued to be used as business premises. By 1957, it had fallen into such disrepair that there were plans to demolish it. Many people did not wish this to happen.

A group of people in Amsterdam campaigned to stop this, and set up the Anne Frank House with the help of Otto Frank.

They prevented the demolition from going ahead. In 1960, it opened the premises at Prinsengracht 263 and 265 to visitors. Not only the Secret Annexe is open to the public, but the other premises are devoted to exhibitions on anti-semitism, National Socialism*, and the Netherlands during the Second World War, as well as displaying the original diary of Anne Frank. Attention is also devoted to contemporary examples of intolerance, racism, discrimination and anti-semitism.

The Anne Frank House in Amsterdam. Every year it is visited by about 600,000 people from all over the world.

Anne Frank's room. There is no longer any furniture in the Secret Annexe, but many traces of the families who went into hiding there remain. For example, in Anne's room, there are the photographs of filmstars which she hung on the walls.

Explanation of terms

Allied Forces

The countries which fought together against Germany, Italy and Japan during the Second World War. The Allies included the United States, England, France and the Soviet Union.

Anti-semitism

Hatred of Jews. Throughout history Jews have often been blamed for things which were no one's fault: failed harvests, diseases and other natural disasters. For centuries, Jews were often mistreated, murdered and banished from their towns or country, simply because they were Jews.

Chanukka

A Jewish winter festival which lasts eight days. Every evening one candle is lit in a nine-branched candle holder. On the first evening one candle is lit, on the second evening two are lit, and so on. The ninth candle is used to light all the other candles. A special game is played with a spinning top and people give each other presents.

Communion

Celebration when a child is accepted into the Catholic faith in church. This event is usually celebrated at home with family visits and presents.

Concentration camp

Camps for prisoners in which the National Socialists interned opponents to their system and people they considered to be inferior, without any form of trial, from 1933-1945. It was almost impossible to escape from a concentration camp. The camps were surrounded by high gates with barbed wire. Usually the wire was electrified. The prisoners lived in the most inhuman conditions. Some of the concentration camps were designated as extermination camps*.

Coupons

In the war the government tried to share articles which were in short supply fairly amongst the population. Coupons were issued for this purpose. You could only buy certain goods with these coupons.

Coupon suppliers

Members of the Resistance who helped to find coupons for people in hiding. Those who were in hiding had no official address and therefore did not receive any coupons.

Deportation

Sending people to a prison or a concentration camp.

Extermination camps

Concentration camps which were specially designed to kill as many people as possible very quickly. There were gas chambers where people were gassed in large groups at a time. The bodies were then burned in incineration furnaces. The extermination camps were built in isolated areas in Poland.

Gestapo

Abbreviation for the Secret State Police. The German secret police force during the occupation.

Going into hiding

Trying to escape the German measures by hiding. During the war, increasing numbers of non-Jews also went into hiding: members of the Resistance for whom things were too dangerous, men who refused to work in Germany, and so on. It is estimated that in the Netherlands between 250,000 and 300,000 people went into hiding for a longer or shorter period.

Illegal, illegality

Illegal means forbidden. It is another word used to describe the Resistance: any actions undertaken against the occupying forces. There were many different forms of Resistance, such as helping people in hiding, armed Resistance and writing, distributing and reading forbidden newspapers.

Invasion

Arrival of a large army. On 6 October 1944, the Allied Forces landed on the French coast in Normandy. Soldiers and equipment were landed in large ships to liberate Europe from the Nazis.

'Kristallnacht'

This is the name of the night of 9-10 November 1938. On that night Nazis throughout Germany destroyed synagogues and Jewish shops. Thousands of Jews were rounded up and sent to concentration camps. The name is a reference to the many windows that were smashed.

Liberal Jews

Jews who felt a link with the traditions of the Jewish religion but who were not devout believers.

National Socialism

The ideas of Hitler and his supporters are known as National Socialism. National Socialists believe in one leader who has total power, and are against democracy. National Socialists are for discrimination and racism, and do not believe that all people are equal.

Nazis

Supporters of National Socialism are known as National Socialists or Nazis. The term Nazi is derived from the German words 'NAtional-soZlalismus'.

NSDAP

The National Socialist German Labour Party. The party was founded in 1920. Its leader was Adolf Hitler.

'Radio Oranje'

Many people secretly listened to the radio broadcasts from London. The families hiding in the Secret Annexe also listened to these broadcasts. Every day there was a special broadcast in Dutch. The station was known as 'Radio Oranje', after the name of the Dutch Royal Family (Oranje-Nassau).

Raid or Razzia

Organized hunting for a group of people. During a raid the Germans would seal off particular streets or a whole district. Everyone in that district was checked. The occupying forces carried out these raids particularly to round up Jews and people who were in hiding. They were immediately arrested and taken away. Often the police would help the military in these raids.

Shorthand

A method for writing very quickly. Instead of writing words, signs and abbreviations are used. People who have to write from dictation very quickly, such as secretaries and journalists, often use shorthand.

SS

Abbreviation for Schutzstaffel. This means a protection unit in German. The SS was a National Socialist military organization with a great deal of power. They were greatly feared for their cruelty. The caps of the SS officers were 'decorated' with a skull.

SS guards

The SS guarded the concentration camps. Throughout Europe, SS officers tortured and murdered men, women and children both in the concentration camps and outside.

Swastika

The swastika was the symbol of the NSDAP*. It was shown everywhere: on buildings, uniforms, letters, stamps, etc. In 1935, the swastika flag became the official flag of Germany.

Synagogue

Place, hall or building where Jews gather together to pray, celebrate and learn from Jewish religious texts.

Yellow Star of David

A six pointed yellow star with the word 'Jew' in the middle. All the Jews in the parts of Europe that were occupied by Germany had to wear this star on their clothes so that it was clearly visible. In the Netherlands this was compulsory from May 1942.

Important dates

Important dates for the Frank family and the other people in hiding

12 May 1889: Otto Frank was born in Frankfurt am Main.

16 january 1900: Edith Holländer was born in Aachen.

12 may 1925: Otto Frank and Edith Holländer's wedding day

16 February 1926: Margot Frank was born in Frankfurt am Main.

Autumn 1927: The Frank family moved to the Marbachweg 307.

12 June 1929: Anne Frank was born in Frankfurt am Main.

March 1931: The Frank family moved to the Ganghofer-strasse 24.

Summer 1933: Edith, Margot and Anne Frank went to stay with grandmother Holländer in Aachen. Otto went to the Netherlands.

15 September 1933: Otto Frank established the company Opekta Werke.

October 1933: Alice Frank-Stern, Anne's grandmother moved to Basel in Switzerland.

5 December 1933: Edith and Margot Frank moved to the Netherlands.

February 1934: Anne Frank left for the Netherlands.

1934: Anne went to the infant class of the Montessori school.

Summer 1937: The Van Pels family fled from Osnabrück to the Netherlands.

1 June 1938: A second company was established: Pectacon BV.

8 December 1938: Fritz Pfeffer fled from Germany to the Netherlands.

March 1939: Grandmother Holländer moved from Aachen to live with the Frank family.

1 December 1940: Otto Frank's company moved to the Prinsengracht 263 in Amsterdam.

8 May 1941: Opekta Werke changed its name to: Handelsver-eniging Gies & Co.

Summer 1941: Anne and Margot went to the Jewish High School in Amsterdam.

January 1942: Grandmother Holländer died.

12 June 1942: Anne Frank was given a diary for her 13th birthday.

5 July 1942: Margot Frank received a call-up card to report for being transported.

6 July 1942: The Frank family went into hiding in the Secret Annexe on the Prinsen-gracht 263 in Amsterdam.

13 July 1942: The Van Pels family (Van Daan) joined the Frank family in the Secret Annexe.

16 November 1942: Fritz Pfeffer (Albert Dussel) moved into the Secret Annexe.

4 August 1944: The Frank family and the other people in hiding were discovered.

8 August 1944: The people who had hidden in the Secret Annexe were taken to the camp in Westerbork.

3 September 1944: They were all taken to the camp at Auschwitz in Poland.

6 September 1944: Arrival in Auschwitz. Hermann van Pels was gassed there a few weeks later.

October 1944: Anne and Margot were taken to the camp in Bergen-Belsen.

20 December 1944: Fritz Pfeffer died in Neuengamme.

6 January 1945: Edith Frank died in Auschwitz.

27 January 1945: Otto Frank was liberated in Auschwitz by the Russian army.

March 1945: Anne and Margot died in Bergen-Belsen.

5 May 1945: Peter Van Pels died in the camp at Mauthausen.

Spring 1945: Mrs. Van Pels died in the camp at Theresien-stadt.

3 June 1945: Otto Frank arrived in Amsterdam.

Summer 1947: The Diary of Anne Frank was published in Dutch.

1952: Otto Frank moved to Basel in Switzerland.

November 1953: Otto Frank married Elfriede Geiringer.

19 August 1980: Otto Frank died in Birsfelden at the age of 91.

The helpers
Bep Voskuijl died on 6 May 1983. Victor Kugler moved to Toronto in Canada in 1955. He died there on 16 December 1981. Johannes Kleiman died on 30 January 1959. Miep and Jan Gies are both living in Amsterdam in 1992.

Further reading

Further reading on Anne Frank and the Second World War

ANNE FRANK

Anne Frank Stichting, *Anne Frank House, A museum with a story*. The Hague, SDU, 1992, 96 p.

Anne Frank Stichting, *Anne Frank in the World 1929-1945*. Amsterdam, Bert Bakker, 1985, 144 p.

Anne Frank Stichting (ed.), *Anne Frank Journal*. The Hague, NBLC. 16 p. This journal is a magazine meant for pupils. It provides a good base for an educational programme about the Second World War, Nazi-ideology and current issues such as the multi-ethnic society and racism and discrimination. A set of Teacher's notes is also available.

Frank, Anne, *The diary of Anne Frank*. London, Pan Books, 1989, 223 p.

Frank, Anne, *The diary of a young girl*. New York, Doubleday, 1989, 237 p.

Frank, Anne, *Anne Frank's tales from the secret annexe*. Middlesex, Penguin, 1986, 144 p.

Gies, Miep, *Anne Frank remembered. The story of the woman who helped to hide the Frank family*. London, Simon & Schuster, 1987, 252 p.

Lindwer, Willy, *The last seven months of Anne Frank*. New York, Pantheon, 1991, 204 p.

The Netherlands State Institute for War Documentation, *The diary of Anne Frank: the critical edition*. New York, Doubleday, 1989, 719 p.

YOUTH LITERATURE

Durlacher, Gerhard, *Stripes in the sky. A wartime memoir*. London, Serpent's Tail, 1991, 106 p.
The author was one of Auschwitz's prisoners and one of its few survivors. This book reflects the authors personal quest to discover the reasons for the passive silence in the face of the mass destruction of European Jewry. (16 years)

Minco, Marga, *Bitter herbs. A little chronicle*. London, Penguin, 1991, 115 p.
The vivid memories of a fugitive Jewish girl in Nazi-occupied Holland. (12 years)

Oberski, Jona, *Childhood*. New York, Doubleday, 1983, 119 p.
The world of a Jewish child during the war and in the period directly after the liberation is portrayed convincingly. The author has managed to recapture the world as seen through the eyes of a child. (13 years)

Orgel, Doris, *The devil in Vienna*. New York, The Dial Press, 1978.
A semi-autobiographical novel about the doomed friendship of two girls - Inge, a Jew, and Liese, a member of the Hitler Youth - in Vienna in 1938. (14 years)

Reiss, Johanna, *The upstairs room*. Middlesex, Penguin, 1979, 159 p.
A book based on the author's own childhood experiences in occupied Holland. For three cramped and frustrating years two girls had to hide in the upstairs room of a remote farmhouse. (12 years)

Schloss, Eva, *Eva's story. A survivor's tale by the step-sister of Anne Frank*. Edgware, Castle-Kent, 1992, 224 p.
In March 1938 the Germans invaded Austria and young Eva fled with her family to Amsterdam. There they hid from the Nazis until they were betrayed in 1944. Together with her mother Eva survived Auschwitz. (14 years)

FURTHER INFORMATION

The Anne Frank Educational Trust is a British Registrated Charity. For more information on the touring exhibition 'Anne Frank in the world' and educational materials contact:
Gillian Walnes
Garden Floor
43 Portland Place
London W1N3A6
071 - 3230696

Anne Frank Center
For more information on the touring exhibition 'Anne Frank in the world' and educational materials contact:
Grayson Covil
106 East 19th Street
4th floor, NY,
New York 10003
212 - 5299532

Registers

Various editions

The various editions of the diary of Anne Frank

In the spring of 1944, Anne Frank heard Minister Bolkestein on Radio Oranje. He said that the Dutch government was planning to publish stories about the war, when it had ended. Anne decided that she wanted to publish her diary after the war. She started to copy her diary onto single sheets of paper. She omitted some parts and improved others. Sometimes she also added sections. At the same time, Anne Frank also continued to write her ordinary diary.

After the war, Miep Gies gave these sheets of Anne's diary to Otto Frank. After giving it a great deal of thought, Otto Frank decided to publish the diary. He compiled a book from the original diary and the version changed by Anne. He left out some of the entries which he thought were not important or interesting. In 1947, the diary was first published under the title 'Het Achterhuis'.

Otto Frank died in 1980. He left all the papers of his daughter's diary to the State of the Netherlands.

Since the 1950s, increasing numbers of people have insisted that the Diary of Anne Frank is a fake. They argued that a child of fifteen could never have written like that. In order to dispel these rumours for once and for all, all the papers of the diary were scientifically examined. This examination showed that there was absolutely no doubt about the diary's authenticity. The results of the examination were published in 1986 in 'The Diaries of Anne Frank'. This work contains (nearly) all the different diary texts which Anne wrote. It also includes a description of the family's background and the facts relating to their arrest and deportation.

Following the edition, 'The Diaries of Anne Frank', a completely new version of 'Het Achterhuis' was published in 1991. This included many entries which Otto Frank had omitted in 1947.

When Anne Frank rewrote her diary with a view to publishing it, she gave false names to the people in hiding with her and the helpers. In the 1947 edition, Otto Frank kept these false names. In the new version of 1991, the people in hiding with Anne kept their false names, but the helpers were given their real names.

These are the false names which Anne gave to the helpers and the other people in hiding with her, followed by their real names.
Mr. Koophuis:
    Johannes Kleiman.
Mr. Kraler:
    Victor Kugler.
Elli Vossen:
    Bep Voskuijl.
Mr. Vossen:
    Mr. Voskuijl.
Miep van Santen:
    Miep Gies.
Henk van Santen:
    Jan Gies.
The Van Daan family:
    the Van Pels family.
Albert Dussel:
    Fritz Pfeffer.

Quotations from the diary in this book, 'Anne Frank', are taken from 'The diary of Anne Frank: the critical edition' (New York, Doubleday, 1989).

Sources of quotations:

All quotations of the diary of Anne Frank:

Netherlands State Institute for War Documentation, *The diary of Anne Frank: the critical edition.* New York, Doubleday 1989, 719 p. Introduced by Harry Paape, Gerrold van der Stroom and David Barnouw; with the summary of the report of the law laboratory, drawn up by H.J.J. Hardy.

Page 41
Quotation: Frank, Anne, *Anne Frank's tales from the secret annexe.* Middlesex, Penguin 1986, p. 25

Page 54/55
Quotations: Lindwer, Willy. *The last seven months of Anne Frank.* New York, Pantheon 1991.

Mrs. Van Amerongen-Frankfoorder: p. 103.
Mrs. Pick-Goslar: p. 27-28.
Mrs. Brandes-Brilleslijper: p. 74.
Mrs. Van Amerongen-Frankfoorder: p. 104.

Page 57
The quotation of Otto Frank is taken from: *Anne Frank 1929-1979.*
Anne Frank Stiftung, Amsterdam. Verlag Lambert Scheiber, Heidelberg 1979, p. 63.

© All texts by Anne Frank: Anne Frank Fonds, Basel.

Origin of photographs:

The photographs have been taken from the following collections:

© **ANP-foto,** p. 46 Diary papers.
Gemeentearchief Amsterdam, p. 16 Merwedeplein, p. 28 Merwedeplein.
Miep Gies, p. 18 Otto Frank and Miep Gies, p. 22 Wedding, p. 26 Photograph, p. 32 Office, p. 35 Menu, Otto Frank and Miep Gies.
Historisches Museum Frankfurt am Main, p. 9 House at Marbachweg, p. 12 Town Hall Frankfurt.
© **Wubbo de Jong,** p. 32 Room of Anne Frank, p. 34 Room of the Van Daans, p. 37 Room of Edith and Otto Frank.
© **Jules Huf,** p. 50 Karl Silberbauer.
© **KLM Luchtfotografie – Schiphol,** p. 30 Aerial photograph.
© **Vereniging Lau Mazirel,** p. 53 Gypsy children.
© **Cas Oorthuys/Stichting Nederlands Fotoarchief,** p. 33 Hiding place.
Opekta Werke, p. 18 Advertising.
Rijksinstituut voor Oorlogsdocumentatie, p. 13 Adolf Hitler, p. 15 Jewish children, p. 20 Children with Star of David, p: 27 (both), p. 33 Children, p. 40 Distribution coupons, p. 50 Headquarters, p. 51 Puls firm, Westerbork, p. 52 photographs Auschwitz, p. 53 Cattle wagon, p. 54 (all), p. 55 (all).

Rode Kruis, The Hague, p. 52 List of names.
© **Spaarnestad Fotoarchief,** p. 13 'Kristallnacht', p. 15 Railway station Naarden, p. 20 Forbidden for Jews.
Stedelijk Beheer Amsterdam, p. 28 Map of Amsterdam
© **Stichting Particam/Maria Austria,** p. 29 Warehouse, p. 35 Cupboard, p. 36 Kleiman and Kugler, p. 38 Attic, p. 42 Window, p. 43 Attic, p. 45 (both), p. 50 Kleiman.

The other photographs can be found in the collection of the Anne Frank House.

For the above mentioned photographs without copyright notice applies:
© **AFF/Anne Frank House, Amsterdam, The Netherlands.**

The Anne Frank House tried to contact those people who have the copyright to photographs. Anyone who believes he has a copyright to illustrations and/or text is requested to contact the Anne Frank House.

Some of the concentration and extermination camps

The first concentration camps were built soon after Hitler came to power in 1933. These were for political prisoners, members of Resistance and people considered to be inferior by the Nazis. Many prisoners were shot or died of hunger and exhaustion.

After the invasion of Poland in 1939, and later also the Soviet Union, hundreds of thousands of Jews were shot dead on the spot.

At the beginning of 1942, the Nazis decided to murder all the Jews in Europe systematically. Concentration camps were built in Poland designed to kill people in large numbers. The Nazis called these 'extermination camps'.

By the end of the Second World War about six million Jews had been murdered.

The map shows how many Jews it is estimated were killed from different countries.

A number of countries are not shown on the map. Jews were also killed from Norway (728), Finland (11), Estonia (1,000) Greece (71,300), Albania (200) and Libya (562).

The countries on this map have the 1939 borders. After the Second World War the borders of some of the countries were changed.

▲ concentration camps

▬ extermination camps

▬ number of Jews who died per country (estimate)

Ⓐ places where the people who hid in the Secret Annexe stayed

SW (NEU

DENMARK
77

THE NETHERLANDS
106,000

NEUENGAMME

▲ RAVENS

BERGEN-BELSEN

▲ SACHSEN

GERMANY
160,000

VUGHT

DORA-MITTELBAU

BUCHENWALD

BELGIUM
24,000

TH

LUXEMBOURG
700

FLOSSENBÜRG

FRANCE
83,000

NATZWEILER

DACHAU

SWITZERLAND
(NEUTRAL)

ITALY
8,000